INTRODUCING
ISSUES WITH
OPPOSING
VIEWPOINTS®

Antibiotics

Mary E. Williams, *Book Editor*

GREENHAVEN PRESS
A part of Gale, Cengage Learning

GALE
CENGAGE Learning·

Detroit • New York • San Francisco • New Haven, Conn • Waterville, Maine • London

GALE
CENGAGE Learning·

Elizabeth Des Chenes, *Director, Content Strategy*
Cynthia Sanner, *Publisher*
Douglas Dentino, *Manager, New Product*

© 2014 Greenhaven Press, a part of Gale, Cengage Learning

WCN: 01-100-101

For more information, contact:
Greenhaven Press
27500 Drake Rd.
Farmington Hills, MI 48331-3535
Or you can visit our Internet site at gale.cengage.com

For product information and technology assistance, contact us at

Gale Customer Support, 1-800-877-4253
For permission to use material from this text or product, submit all requests online at
www.cengage.com/permissions

Further permissions questions can be e-mailed to permissionrequest@cengage.com

Articles in Greenhaven Press anthologies are often edited for length to meet page requirements. In addition, original titles of these works are changed to clearly present the main thesis and to explicitly indicate the author's opinion. Every effort is made to ensure that Greenhaven Press accurately reflects the original intent of the authors. Every effort has been made to trace the owners of copyrighted material.

Cover image © lenetstan/Shutterstock.com.

LIBRARY OF CONGRESS CATALOGING-IN-PUBLICATION DATA

Antibiotics / Mary E. Williams, book editor.
    pages cm. -- (Introducing issues with opposing viewpoints)
  Summary: "Antibiotics: Introducing Issues with Opposing Viewpoints is a series that examines current issues from different viewpoints, set up in a pro/con format"-- Provided by publisher.
  Includes bibliographical references and index.
  ISBN 978-0-7377-6919-7 (hardback)
  1. Antibiotics--Juvenile literature. 2. Drug resistance in microorganisms--Juvenile literature. I. Williams, Mary E., 1960-
  RM267.A5213 2013
  615.3'29--dc23
                                                                    2013033244

Printed in the United States of America
1 2 3 4 5 6 7 18 17 16 15 14

Contents

Foreword

Indulging in a wide spectrum of ideas, beliefs, and perspectives is a critical cornerstone of democracy. After all, it is often debates over differences of opinion, such as whether to legalize abortion, how to treat prisoners, or when to enact the death penalty, that shape our society and drive it forward. Such diversity of thought is frequently regarded as the hallmark of a healthy and civilized culture. As the Reverend Clifford Schutjer of the First Congregational Church in Mansfield, Ohio, declared in a 2001 sermon, "Surrounding oneself with only like-minded people, restricting what we listen to or read only to what we find agreeable is irresponsible. Refusing to entertain doubts once we make up our minds is a subtle but deadly form of arrogance." With this advice in mind, Introducing Issues with Opposing Viewpoints books aim to open readers' minds to the critically divergent views that comprise our world's most important debates.

Introducing Issues with Opposing Viewpoints simplifies for students the enormous and often overwhelming mass of material now available via print and electronic media. Collected in every volume is an array of opinions that captures the essence of a particular controversy or topic. Introducing Issues with Opposing Viewpoints books embody the spirit of nineteenth-century journalist Charles A. Dana's axiom: "Fight for your opinions, but do not believe that they contain the whole truth, or the only truth." Absorbing such contrasting opinions teaches students to analyze the strength of an argument and compare it to its opposition. From this process readers can inform and strengthen their own opinions, or be exposed to new information that will change their minds. Introducing Issues with Opposing Viewpoints is a mosaic of different voices. The authors are statesmen, pundits, academics, journalists, corporations, and ordinary people who have felt compelled to share their experiences and ideas in a public forum. Their words have been collected from newspapers, journals, books, speeches, interviews, and the Internet, the fastest growing body of opinionated material in the world.

Introducing Issues with Opposing Viewpoints shares many of the well-known features of its critically acclaimed parent series, Opposing Viewpoints. The articles are presented in a pro/con format, allowing readers to absorb divergent perspectives side by side. Active reading questions preface each viewpoint, requiring the student to approach the material thoughtfully and carefully. Useful charts, graphs, and cartoons supplement each article. A thorough introduction provides readers with crucial background on an issue. An annotated bibliography points the reader toward articles, books, and websites that contain additional information on the topic. An appendix of organizations to contact contains a wide variety of charities, nonprofit organizations, political groups, and private enterprises that each hold a position on the issue at hand. Finally, a comprehensive index allows readers to locate content quickly and efficiently.

Introducing Issues with Opposing Viewpoints is also significantly different from Opposing Viewpoints. As the series title implies, its presentation will help introduce students to the concept of opposing viewpoints and learn to use this material to aid in critical writing and debate. The series' four-color, accessible format makes the books attractive and inviting to readers of all levels. In addition, each viewpoint has been carefully edited to maximize a reader's understanding of the content. Short but thorough viewpoints capture the essence of an argument. A substantial, thought-provoking essay question placed at the end of each viewpoint asks the student to further investigate the issues raised in the viewpoint, compare and contrast two authors' arguments, or consider how one might go about forming an opinion on the topic at hand. Each viewpoint contains sidebars that include at-a-glance information and handy statistics. A Facts About section located in the back of the book further supplies students with relevant facts and figures.

Following in the tradition of the Opposing Viewpoints series, Greenhaven Press continues to provide readers with invaluable exposure to the controversial issues that shape our world. As John Stuart Mill once wrote: "The only way in which a human being can make some approach to knowing the whole of a subject is by hearing what can be said about it by persons of every variety of opinion and studying all modes in which it can be looked at by every character of mind. No wise man ever acquired his wisdom in any mode but this." It is to this principle that Introducing Issues with Opposing Viewpoints books are dedicated.

Introduction

"One of the great medical advances of the last century, antibiotics, is at risk of being lost."

—*Washington Post* editorial, July 11, 2012

In 2013 Sally Davies, the chief medical officer for Britain's Department of Health, expressed deep concern about the future of one of humanity's most valuable medicines: antibiotics. Speaking before a parliamentary science and technology committee, she warned that microbes' growing resistance to antibiotics could lead to an "apocalyptic scenario"[1] in which people die from common, once-curable infections. For example, the *Staphylococcus* ("staph") bacterium—the cause of many skin and soft-tissue infections—has become resistant to penicillin. Eighty percent of gonorrhea cases are resistant to tetracycline, and there is currently only one other antibiotic that can cure that disease. Antibiotics are also losing their effectiveness against tuberculosis, which kills at least 150,000 people worldwide each year. With almost no new anti-infective "wonder drugs" being developed, bacterial resistance to antibiotics is a greater threat to humanity than global warming, Davies contends.

The first medical antibiotic, penicillin—derived from mold—was discovered in 1928 and became widely available in England and the United States during the 1940s. As the first family of drugs that effectively treated syphilis and infections caused by strep and staph bacteria, penicillin and other antibiotics transformed modern medicine. Not only did they cure previously serious illnesses, their anti-infective properties also allowed physicians to perform successful heart surgeries, organ transplants, cancer therapies, and other lifesaving interventions. By the late 1950s, however, a strain of staph bacteria had developed an enzyme that counteracted penicillin. Physicians turned to an alternate penicillin, methicillin, to kill this strain. Then in 1960, scientists discovered a strain of staph that had become resistant to methicillin as well. The wide use of antibiotics was apparently pushing bacteria to evolve and produce antibiotic-resistant variants, sometimes referred to as "superbugs." As epidemiologist John Jernigan explains, "We can always expect antibiotic resistance to follow antibiotic use, surely as night follows day."[2] Science reporter Jeremy Manier explains further: "Antibiotics shove bacteria into an evolutionary corner, weeding out the vulnerable varieties and offering an opportunity to strains that have picked up key defensive traits."[3]

The problem worsens when antibiotics are overused or misused. Antibiotics cannot kill viruses, including the various flu viruses, but doctors sometimes prescribe these drugs for patients in case they come down with a bacterial infection, such as pneumonia, *after* a viral illness. However, many people mistakenly believe that antibiotics will help them get over a virus, and they end up taking these medicines when they do not need them. This type of misuse kills the beneficial bacteria that help to keep superbugs under control—and allows these strains of resistant bacteria to multiply further. Even patients who take antibiotics for bacterial infections can make the situation worse if they do not take their full course of medicine. "When patients stop taking a dose midway, weaker bugs are knocked out, leaving stronger ones behind to be passed along,"[4] explains researcher Ramanan Laxminarayan.

Some experts also maintain that the agricultural industry contributes to the development of antibiotic-resistant bacteria. On large factory farms, cows, pigs, and chickens are fed low levels of antibiotics to prevent the infections that can occur in crowded conditions. These low levels of antibiotics, many say, expose bacteria to doses of drugs that do not kill them off completely. Instead, the bacteria become more immune to antibiotics and can spread to humans through the food supply. This, in turn, increases the chances for serious, hard-to-treat infections to emerge in human populations.

While many in the scientific and medical communities are voicing alarm about the threat of antibiotic-resistant bacteria, not all have given up hope on finding and developing new antibacterial medicines. In 2012 researchers discovered an ancient species of naturally resistant bacteria in the Lechuguilla Cave in New Mexico. This strain—harmless to humans—is resistant to many medical antibiotics even though it has been isolated from human contact for more than 4 million years. This is a significant finding, because it reveals that bacterial resistance is not solely a human-made phenomenon. "Our study shows that antibiotic resistance is hard-wired into bacteria," says investigator Gerry Wright, director of the Institute for Infectious Disease Research. Each bacterium actually creates its own antibiotic substances to help them fight off other bacteria. "This has important clinical implications," Wright explains, because "it suggests that there are far more antibiotics in the environment that could be found and used to treat currently untreatable infections."[5] Thus, many natural antibiotics are yet to be discovered, and some of them could be developed into medicines for humans.

One possible source of new antibiotics is the fluid that frogs secrete from their skin. For more than a decade, English researcher John Michael Conlon has collected hundreds of samples of frog-skin secretions from around the world. Frogs live in warm, moist environments and have spent millions of years fighting off microbes, Conlon points out. Thus far, after analyzing two hundred such secretions, Conlon's research team has discovered more than one hundred antibacterial substances. Cockroach brains and lichens (fungi that grow with algae) also show powerful antibiotic potential. Such investigations remain challenging, however—research is slow and receives little support from drug companies. Moreover, it will be trickier to develop medicines to combat superbugs that are resistant to multiple antibiotics. As research chemist John Sorensen puts it, "We're looking for a new class of antibiotics. We would win no prizes for finding more penicillin."[6]

Creating more effective antibiotics in many ways resembles an arms race, because any new drugs will likely be met with more powerful resistance from bacteria in the future. Thus, many health professionals are calling for better supervision of today's antibiotics, with campaigns that teach physicians to limit their prescriptions of these medicines and laws that discourage the overuse of antibiotics in agriculture. The authors in *Introducing Issues with Opposing Viewpoints: Antibiotics* examine these and other debates surrounding the benefits and dangers of these powerful medicines.

Notes

1. Quoted in Lin Edwards, "Expert Warning: Resistance to Antibiotics to Be Apocalyptic," Medicalxpress.com, January 25, 2013. http://medicalxpress.com/news/2013-01-expert-resistance-antibiotics -apocalyptic.html.

2. Quoted in Jeremy Manier, "How Staph Became Drug-Resistant Threat," *Chicago Tribune*, November 4, 2007. http://articles.chicago tribune.com/2007-11-04/news/0711030893_1_mrsa-superbug -drug-resistant.

3. Manier, "How Staph Became Drug-Resistant Threat."

4. Quoted in Kate Lunau, *Maclean's*, "Superbug: Meet Your Maker: Frogs Evolved to Fight Off Microbes. They May Also Provide Us with the Next Class of Antibiotics," September 27, 2010. www2 .macleans.ca/2010/09/16/superbug-meet-your-maker.

5. Quoted in Sheryl Ubelacker, "Ancient Cave Discovery Unlocks Secrets of Superbugs," *Globe and Mail* (Toronto, ON), April 12, 2012. www.theglobeandmail.com/life/health-and-fitness/ancient-cave -discovery-unlocks-secrets-of-superbugs/article4099765.

6. Quoted in Lunau, "Superbug."

Chapter 1

Are Antibiotics Harmful?

Because of their possible side effects and overuse, antibiotics have become controversial.

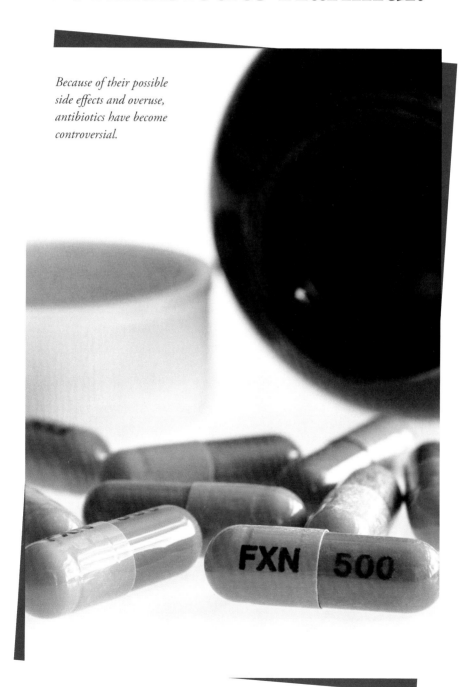

FXN 500

Viewpoint

1

Antibiotics Are Beneficial

Brian Hoyle

In the following selection medical writer Brian Hoyle explores the history and nature of antibacterial drugs. For thousands of years, he notes, humans have treated infections with molds and plants that have antibacterial properties; however, the antibiotic era really began early in the twentieth century with a treatment for syphilis, a sexually transmitted disease caused by a bacterium. Since then, many new classes of antibiotics have been developed, including cephalosporins, quinolones, and others. Some antibiotics work by destroying bacterial membranes; others disrupt protein production within bacteria; still others impair bacterial DNA.

Antibiotics have been highly successful in treating infectious diseases and curbing epidemics of cholera, plague, and yellow fever, Hoyle asserts. But the overuse of these drugs has also led to the development of antibiotic-resistant bacteria, causing stronger forms of once-conquered diseases to emerge. He expects that these emerging illnesses will require the creation of more-effective antibiotics.

> *"Every year, antibiotics continue to save millions of lives around the world."*

AS YOU READ, CONSIDER THE FOLLOWING QUESTIONS:
1. What is the difference between bacteriostatic and bactericidal drugs, according to the author?
2. According to Hoyle, how do broad-spectrum antibiotics differ from narrow-spectrum antibiotics?
3. When did scientists first observe bacterial resistance to antibiotics, according to the author?

Antibacterial drugs stop bacterial infections in two ways: they prevent bacteria from dividing and increasing in number, or they kill the bacteria. The former drugs, which prevent bacteria from increasing in number but do not kill the bacteria, are termed bacteriostatic drugs. The latter, which kill the infectious bacteria, are known as bactericidal drugs. Both types of drugs can stop an infection.

The terms *antibacterial drugs* and *antibiotics* are often used interchangeably. Though the most common antibacterial drugs are the many types of antibiotics, other compounds can also be considered antibacterial. One example is alcohol, which kills bacteria by dissolving the cell membrane. Another example is carbolic acid, which was famously used by Joseph Lister (1827–1912) in the mid-nineteenth century as a spray to prevent bacterial contamination of wounds during operations. Antibacterial agents such as alcohol and carbolic acid are more accurately considered disinfectants, chemicals that kill or inactivate bacteria on surfaces and instruments, rather than antibiotics, which are generally taken internally and can create resistant strains of bacteria.

The History of Antibiotics

The use of antibacterial drugs is ancient. Thousands of years ago, although the scientific basis of infection and its treatment was unknown, infections were sometimes successfully treated with molds and plants. Centuries later, the production of antibiotics by some species of molds and plants was discovered. One argument against the large-scale deforestation of regions, such as the Amazon basin, is that there are likely still many antibiotic-producing molds and plants yet to be discovered.

The antibiotic era began in the first decade of the twentieth century, when Paul Ehrlich (1854–1915) discovered a compound that proved to be an effective treatment for syphilis. In 1928, Sir Alexander Fleming (1881–1955) discovered the antibiotic penicillin. With recognition of the compound's prowess in killing a wide variety of bacteria, interest in antibiotics soared. In 1941, Selman Waksman (1888–1973) coined the term *antibiotic*. In the ensuing decades, much work focused on the discovery of new antibiotics from natural sources, the laboratory alteration of existing compounds to increase their potency (and, later, to combat the problem of antibiotic resistance), and the synthesis of entirely new antibiotics.

Antibiotics kill bacteria in a variety of ways. Some alter the structure of the bacteria so that the bacteria become structurally weakened and unable to withstand physical stresses, such as pressure, with the result that the bacteria explode. Other antibiotics halt the production of various proteins in a number of ways: inhibiting the decoding of the genes specifying the proteins (transcriptional inhibition); blocking the production of the proteins following the production of the genetic message, messenger ribonucleic acid (mRNA, in a process termed *translational inhibition*); blocking the movement of the manufactured protein to its final location in the bacterium; or blocking the import of compounds that are crucial to the continued survival of the bacterium.

Classes of Antibiotics

Some antibiotics—described as broad-spectrum—are effective against many different bacteria. Other antibiotics—described as narrow-spectrum—are very specific in their action and, as a result, affect fewer bacteria.

Penicillin is the classic example of a class of antibiotics known as beta-lactam antibiotics. The term *beta-lactam* refers to the ring structure that is the backbone of these antibiotics. Other classes of antibiotics, which are based on the structure and/or the mechanism of action of the antibiotic, are tetracyclines, rifamycins, quinolones, aminoglycosides, and sulphonamides.

How Antibiotics Kill Bacteria

Beta-lactam antibiotics kill bacteria by altering the construction of a portion of the bacterial membrane called the peptidoglycan.

The antibiotic era began in the first decade of the twentieth century, when Paul Ehrlich (pictured) (1854–1915) discovered a compound that proved to be an effective treatment for syphilis.

This component is a thin layer located between the inner and outer membranes of Gram-negative bacteria (an example is *Escherichia coli* [*E. coli*]) and a much thicker layer in Gram-positive bacteria (an example is *Bacillus anthracis*, the bacterium that causes anthrax). The peptidoglycan is a tennis racket–like mesh of sugar molecules and other compounds that is very strong when intact. This network has to expand to accommodate the growth of the bacteria. This is done by introducing breaks in the peptidoglycan so that newly made material can be inserted and incorporated into the existing network, cross-linking the newly inserted material with the older material. Beta-lactam antibiotics disrupt the final cross-linking step by inhibiting the activity of enzymes called penicillin-binding proteins, which are the enzymes that catalyze the cross-linkage. Other enzymes called autolysins also are released. The autolysins

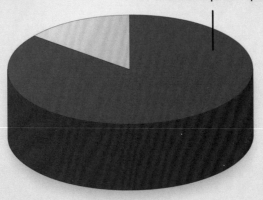

86% of Americans know that
they should take the full course
of antibiotic prescriptions

Taken from: Michelle Castillo. *CBS News*, November 13, 2012.

degrade the exposed peptidoglycan at the sites that are defectively cross-linked. The result is the weakening of the peptidoglycan layer, which causes the bacterium to essentially self-destruct.

Another class of antibiotics with a mode of action similar to the beta-lactam antibiotics are the cephalosporins. There have been various versions, or generations, of cephalosporins that have improved the ability of these antibiotics to withstand enzyme breakdown. The latest cephalosporins are the fourth generation of these antibiotics.

Aminoglycoside antibiotics bind to certain regions of the cellular structure called ribosomes. Ribosomes are responsible for decoding the information contained in mRNA to produce proteins. By binding to the ribosome, aminoglycoside antibiotics disrupt protein production, which is often lethal for the bacterium.

As a final example, quinolone antibiotics impair an enzyme that unwinds the double helix of deoxyribonucleic acid (DNA). This unwinding must occur so that the genetic information can be used to make proteins and other bacterial components. These antibiotics kill bacteria at the genetic level.

Impacts and Issues

Every year, antibiotics continue to save millions of lives around the world. In less developed regions, where access to medical care can be limited, campaigns by the World Health Organization (WHO) and other agencies to distribute antibiotics have been invaluable in the response to epidemics of diseases such as cholera, plague, and yellow fever.

The discovery and manufacture of antibiotics continues. Screening of samples to uncover antibacterial properties has been automated; thousands of samples can be processed each day. Furthermore, the increased knowledge of the molecular details of the active sites of antibiotics and the ability to target specific regions have been exploited in the design of new antibiotics.

Bacterial Resistance

In the decades after pencillin's discovery and use, many different antibiotics were discovered or synthesized and introduced for use. The control of bacterial infections became so routine that it appeared infectious diseases would become a problem of the past. However, that optimism has proven to be premature. Instead, some bacteria have developed resistance to a number of antibiotics. For example, bacterial resistance was first observed only about three years after the commercial introduction and widespread use of penicillin in the late 1940s. Penicillin-resistant staphylococcus bacteria were reported in 1944, and, by the 1950s, a penicillin-resistant strain of *Staphylococcus aureus* became a

FAST FACT

Researcher John Conlon has discovered that frog skin secretes over a hundred antimicrobial substances that someday could be used in a new class of antibiotics.

worldwide problem in hospitals. By the 1960s, most staphylococci were resistant to penicillin. Two decades ago it was rare to encounter methicillin-resistant *S. aureus* (MRSa). [Today], MRSa is a daily concern of a hospital's infection control challenge.

The effectiveness of an antibiotic to which bacteria have developed resistance can sometimes be restored by slightly modifying a chemical group of antibiotic. For example, the antibiotics ampicillin and amoxicillin are variants of penicillin. However, this strategy usually produces only a short-term benefit, since resistance to the altered antibiotic also develops.

Misuse of Antibiotics

One factor contributing to the growth of antibiotic resistance is the overuse or misuse of antibiotics. All the bacteria responsible for an infection may not be killed if an insufficient concentration of an antibiotic is used or if antibiotic therapy is stopped before the prescription has been used completely. The surviving bacteria may possess resistance to the antibiotic, which can sometimes be passed on to other bacteria. For example, tuberculosis has re-emerged as a significant health problem, especially for people whose immune systems are compromised, since the tuberculosis bacteria have developed resistance to the antibiotics used to treat them.

Acinetobacter baumannii is another bacterium that has developed resistance to many antibiotics. This bacterium is normally found in soil and water, and so is commonly encountered. While *Acinetobacter baumannii* infections were once confined to hospitals, where they accounted for about 80% of all nosocomial (hospital-acquired) infections, the bacterium now has become a growing problem for the military. Over 200 U.S. soldiers wounded in Iraq since 2003 have developed serious infections caused by multi-resistant *A. baumannii*, and military physicians have few treatment options for these infections.

New antibacterial drugs are expected to produce blockbuster sales for their manufacturers, as emerging resistant organisms push the development of new and efficient antibiotics into the forefront.

EVALUATING THE AUTHOR'S ARGUMENTS:

At the end of this selection, Brian Hoyle maintains that new and efficient antibiotics will likely be developed. Yet, earlier in his essay he points out that bacteria frequently develop resistance to an antibiotic soon after its creation. Does that fact contradict his optimistic conclusion? Why or why not?

Antibiotic Side Effects Can Be Harmful

"Several fluoroquinolones have been taken off the market due to severe adverse reactions."

Carey Purcell

The fluoroquinolones—one class of antibiotics—has caused severe side effects, poisonings, and deaths in thousands of people, reports Carey Purcell in the following selection. Adverse reactions have included hallucinations, seizures, tendon ruptures, and brain damage—symptoms that may not develop until long after a patient has finished taking the antibiotics. This issue has not received much media coverage, notes Purcell, and physicians are often unaware of the dangers these drugs pose. She concludes that patients need to protect themselves by doing their own research on the medicines prescribed for them. Purcell is a writer, reporter, and critic based in New York.

AS YOU READ, CONSIDER THE FOLLOWING QUESTIONS:
1. According to the author, why is there uncertainty about the number of people who have been poisoned by fluoroquinolones?
2. In the opinion of David Fuller, cited by Purcell, what makes fluoroquinolone antibiotics so harmful?
3. What is the major problem with studies published in medical journals, according to anesthesiologist Todd Plumb, as cited by the author?

B obby Grozier was on top of the world before he took the pills. A senior software adviser for a Fortune 500 company based in Manhattan, he earned a great salary and was happily married with a young daughter. That changed when he was prescribed a toxic combination of drugs to treat lingering symptoms of what his doctor thought was prostatitis. Ten years later, he suffers from permanent brain damage, is on disability and has lost more than $3 million in medical costs and income.

Grozier was prescribed a combination of Ciprofloxacin and Vioxx, a nonsteroidal anti-inflammatory drug. Shortly after taking the medicine his ears began to ring. He called Bayer, the company that produces Ciprofloxacin, and reported his symptoms to a pharmacist who told him to keep taking the drug to get the full effect.

Shortly after Grozier stopped taking the prescriptions, he suffered a psychotic episode. He had difficulty breathing, experienced hallucinations, and was barely able to call his mother to ask her to take him to the hospital.

"Things in my ears were resonating like I was in an echo chamber," Grozier said. "And everything was wavy . . . it was unbearable. I really thought I had a heart attack and was dying."

At the hospital, Grozier was given a sedative. The doctor he spoke with blamed the episode on irritable bowel syndrome, wrote him a prescription for Xanax [an antianxiety drug] and sent him home. But his symptoms steadily worsened. He experienced numerous petite mal seizures [mild seizures with diminished awareness], was unable to bathe himself and suffered from severe anxiety.

"I was praying to God to take my life, let me die," Grozier said. "It was unbearable."

Medication Poisoning

After researching his symptoms online, Grozier concluded that he had been poisoned by the medications his doctor prescribed. Ciprofloxacin is a fluoroquinolone, an antibiotic used to treat bacterial infections in many different parts of the body. Fluoroquinolones include Ciprofloxacin, Levofloxacin and Levaquin, as well as many other drugs. Fluoroquinolone poisoning is a little-known reaction to the drug. Symptoms include central nervous system (CNS) toxicity, phototoxicity [a rash set off by light], cardiotoxicity [heart problems], arthropathy [joint pain] and tendon rupture. Several fluoroquinolones have been taken off the market due to severe adverse reactions, but these instances are few and often result in long legal battles.

The actual amount of poisonings that occur due to floroquinolones is uncertain. Some consider the occurrence to be rare while others say it is far more common than many realize. The lack of recorded cases is due to several factors. Often people do not realize that they have been poisoned, or their doctors do not credit the symptoms to the medication, partly due to the delayed toxicity. Patients can react to the drugs weeks or months after they are prescribed and patients and doctors do not make a connection between the drugs and the symptoms.

Another reason the condition is often unrecognizable is due to its lack of visible physical symptoms. One victim of the poisoning said it is often referred to as "the invisible illness," saying, "[people] look at you and think you're normal because there's no open wound or cast . . . [but] on the inside our nerves are damaged, our tendons are damaged, certain receptors in the brain are not functioning properly."

While stories about floroquinolone poisoning have been published in the Inter Press Service News Agency, the Associated Press and numerous medical journals, the topic is not reported on frequently in the media, and people tend to be skeptical when first learning about it. This lack of knowledge has caused many sufferers to become activists, helping to educate people about the topic. . . .

> **FAST FACT**
>
> Side effects of antibiotics can include nausea, vomiting, diarrhea, rash, headache, lethargy, dizziness, and photosensitivity, to name just a few.

Other Adverse Reactions

John Fratti, a former pharmaceutical sales representative, suffered a severe adverse reaction to Levaquin in 2005. He has tried to increase awareness of the poisoning, attempting to share knowledge about the drugs' effects. Fratti possesses a Freedom of Information report on Levaquin that he requested from the FDA [Food and Drug

Administration], which shows there have been 1,015 death outcomes and 14,796 individual safety reports resulting from the drug.

After contacting the Office of Special Health Issues and meeting with FDA officials to discuss the dangers of Levaquin, Fratti was hired by the agency, serving part-time as an FDA patient representative for drug safety. Increasing awareness about floroquinolone poisoning is crucial to many patients because doctors are often unaware of the condition and attribute the symptoms to stress, depression or another infection. Many patients communicate with each other online. . . .

[David] Fuller took Floxin to treat pneumonia in 1986 and suffered a heart attack and a blow to his Achilles tendon. In the '90s, he took Ciprofloxacin for a sinus infection and has almost completely lost his vision and developed a kidney stone as well as experiencing serious damage to his joints. He diagnosed himself after reading articles online.

"I'm pretty much blind," he said. "Prior to this, I didn't even wear glasses. My hips are going to have to be replaced. My hands are like claws—I can barely bend my fingers. I had to have root canals, and I had teeth break off and fall out of my mouth when I was brushing."
. . .

Fuller said direct toxicity and DNA damage are two reasons floroquinolones are harmful to so many people. "These drugs change the blueprint by which the replacement cells are made. Now you've got defective cells making more defective cells. If the body can recover from it, you'll get better, but if the damage is so massive the body can't recover, you're permanently disabled."

A Doctor's Story

Anesthesiologist Todd Plumb was prescribed Levaquin in 2006. His symptoms included skin burning, profound insomnia and agitation, elevated liver enzymes and numerous issues with his gastrointestinal tract as well as severe numbness and burning pain in his extremities. He described the full onset and progression of neuropathy [nerve pain] as similar to what cancer patients experience when going through chemotherapy.

Plumb, who had never heard of fluoroquinolone poisoning during his years as an emergency room doctor and anesthesiologist, went to

Common Side Effects of Antibiotics

Antibiotic class	Antibiotic class members	Side effects
Penicillins	penicillin, amoxicillin, ampicillin	rash, diarrhea, abdominal pain, nausea, vomiting, fever, allergic reactions
Cephalosporins	cephalexin, cefaclor, cefuroxime	rash, diarrhea, allergic reactions, serum sickness, yeast infections
Macrolides	erythromycin, azithromycin, clarithromycin	abdominal pain, diarrhea, anorexia, nausea, vomiting, taste alterations
Sulfonamides	trimethropin/sulfamethoxazole, sufadiazine	nausea, vomiting, diarrhea, anorexia, abdominal pain, rash, light sensitivity, headache, dizziness
Tetracyclines	tetracycline, doxycycline, minocycline	nausea, vomiting, diarrhea, anorexia, abdominal pain, light sensitivity, tooth discoloration
Quinolones	ciproflaxin, levofloxacin, moxifloxacin	nausea, vomiting, diarrhea, abdominal pain, headache, lethargy, insomnia, light sensitivity
Glycopeptides	vancomycin, televancin	flushing, low blood pressure, itching, phlebitis, taste alteration, nausea, vomiting, headache
Aminoglycocides	gentamicin, tobramycin, amikacin	kidney toxicity, hearing loss, dizziness, nausea, vomiting, involuntary eye movements
Carbapenems	meropenem, ertapenem, doripenem	diarrhea, nausea, vomiting, headache, rash, liver toxicity, elevated white blood cells
Antituberculosis agents	rifampin, rifabutin, isoniazid, pyrazinamide	diarrhea, nausea, vomiting, anemia, liver toxicity, headache, nerve pain, dizziness

Taken from: Drugs.com. "Common Side Effects, Allergies, and Reaction to Antibiotics." www.drugs.com.

15 doctors and spent a week in the Mayo Clinic, attempting to find a diagnosis. He also learned about fluoroquinolone poisoning online.

"You'll see the same story repeated over and over again," he said. "Joint and tendon pain. Tendon rupture. Severe extremity pain. And no one believes them."

The antibiotic Ciprofloxacin has been known to cause adverse side effects such as hallucinations.

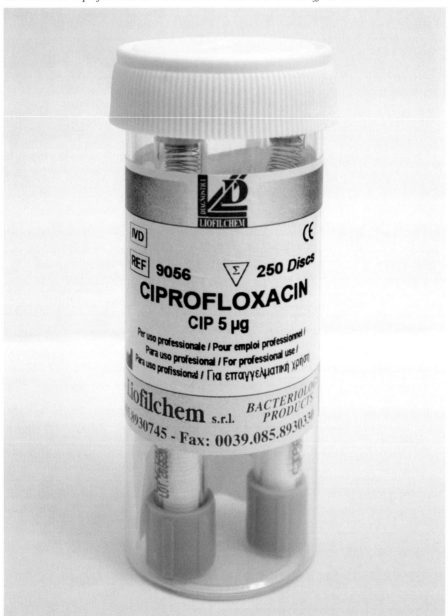

The disbelief, according to Plumb, is due in part to the structure of the health care system, as doctors are taught to have faith in the medicines they prescribe their patients.

"It's like losing faith in your religion," Plumb said. "I was in their camp before it happened to me. I'd had several people complain to me about problems with Cipro. I thought it was a safe medication that worked pretty well. I didn't want to feel myself that I was doing harm to patients."

Bias in Medical Research

Plumb attributes some of this attitude to studies that are published in medical journals, saying almost every study of a drug shows a beneficial outcome.

"The FDA doesn't do the research on the drug," he said. "The research and development and presentation of that is left to the drug companies themselves. And they can alter and change and present the drug in the best way possible."

He credits this partially to the fact that drug companies purchase advertising in medical journals. "Every reputable medical journal in America is funded by drug company advertising. Journals wouldn't get out to doctors unless drugs were advertised in journals.

"It's a culture of drug companies holding all the sway," Plumb continued. "They pay for everything. Even the way the information is dispersed to physicians. If you look at a journal and count how many pages are drug company advertisements and how many are studies, the drug companies outweigh the studies." . . .

Levaquin Lawsuit

In 2008, Johnson & Johnson's drug Levaquin went on trial for causing tendon damage. *Schedin v. Johnson & Johnson* was held in federal court in Minneapolis. John Schedin, 82, filed the suit, claiming he ruptured the Achilles tendons in both feet after taking Levaquin. He claims Johnson & Johnson and its Ortho-McNeil-Janssen Pharmaceuticals unit did not warn doctors and patients of the drug's association with tendon damage. Schedin won the case and was awarded damages of $700,000.

This case is the first trial of more than 2,600 claims in U.S. courts alleging that Levaquin causes tendon damage. In 2008, the FDA required an upgraded warning on tendon damage posed by Levaquin and similar drugs. The black box warning [printed on the package] was required for all fluoroquinolones in July 2008. . . .

In order to increase awareness about fluoroquinolones, Plumb said many aspects of the system are in need of change, including the education received in medical schools. He said very few continuing education courses have much to do with the pharmacy, and if they do, a doctor presents pharmaceutical research in a positive light. . . .

Patients Must Do Their Own Research

Until changes are put into place at the FDA, people can make an effort to ensure their own safety by researching medications on their own.

"A lot of people think the FDA is out there doing their own rigorous studies on the safety and efficacy of drugs and that's not the case. They rely on the information supplied to them by pharmaceutical companies," Fratti said. "Doctors are fed a lot of propaganda from drug reps, and they are influenced in a way that may not be best for the patients. Patients should not blindly put their trust in doctors. I think patients need to be their own health advocates today and do their own research."

EVALUATING THE AUTHOR'S ARGUMENTS:

Carey Purcell argues that some common antibiotics can cause severe and long-term side effects. Moreover, she contends that consumers cannot trust their doctors or the Food and Drug Administration to give them accurate information about these medicines. She suggests that patients must be their own advocates and do their own research before taking these drugs. Do you agree? Explain your answer.

The Use of Antibiotics on Factory Farms Is Harmful

"If we do not change the way we produce meat and poultry . . . we will run out of effective antibiotics."

Deseret News

The farming and food industries must stop overusing antibiotics, argues the *Deseret News* in the following viewpoint. Overexposure to antibiotics has created drug-resistant bacteria that can cause unbeatable and potentially deadly infections. While consumers have become more aware of the need to use antibiotics sparingly, many farms still rely on antibiotics to fatten up animals for slaughter. In the opinion of the *Deseret News,* using antibiotics for anything other than bacterial illnesses is dangerous and irresponsible. Policy makers must find ways to regulate antibiotics before they all become ineffective, the author concludes. The *Deseret News* is a daily newspaper in Salt Lake City, Utah.

AS YOU READ, CONSIDER THE FOLLOWING QUESTIONS:

1. According to the World Health Organization, as cited by the author, how many people in the European Union die of antibiotic-resistant infections each year?
2. How often is an American consumer's meat purchase likely to contain drug-resistant bacteria, according to the *Deseret News*?
3. As stated by the author, what country has successfully reduced antibiotic use in farm animals?

German officials have determined that contaminated vegetable sprouts are to blame for a massive E. coli outbreak that has killed at least 30 people and sickened thousands more.

This strain of the E. coli bacteria is new, and it is ominously resistant to nearly all antibiotics. It is true that antibiotics are not being used to treat the outbreak because these particular bacteria contain toxins that would be released as the drugs killed the bacteria. But it is also true that overuse of antibiotics created the strain in the first place.

How Bacteria Develop Resistance

Bacteria develop resistance to antibiotics through natural selection. As they are exposed to antibiotics, those with immunities survive and pass their resistance on to the next generation of bacteria. And if bacteria like E. coli are overexposed to antibiotics, they develop resistance to antibiotics more quickly than researchers can develop new antibiotics.

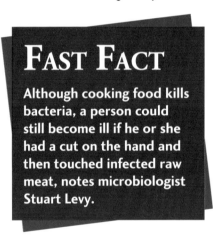

As the current epidemic illustrates, this is not a hypothetical situation. The World Health Organization estimates that in the European Union alone, more than 25,000 people die of antibiotic resistant bacterial infections each year.

It is imperative that antibiotics are used sparingly and only to treat infections; otherwise, they will lose their efficacy completely.

FAST FACT

Although cooking food kills bacteria, a person could still become ill if he or she had a cut on the hand and then touched infected raw meat, notes microbiologist Stuart Levy.

Misuse of Antibiotics in the Food Industry

Thanks to public health campaigns, most people know that antibiotics should be used against bacterial infections and not viruses. What most people don't know is that antibiotics are most overused not in doctor's offices, but in the food industry, where they are widely used to fatten up animals for slaughter—not just to treat illness.

Because of this, antibiotic resistance is so high today that the average U.S. consumer has a one-in-four chance of bringing a multi-drug-resistant strain of staph into the kitchen each time he purchases tur-

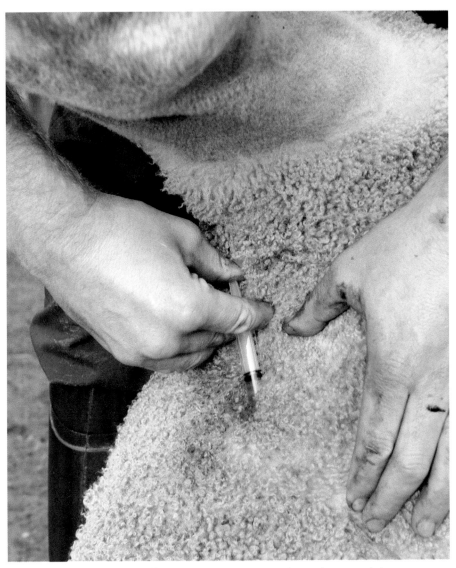

A vet injects a sheep with antibiotics. Overexposure to antibiotics has created drug-resistant bacteria that can cause untreatable and potentially deadly infections.

key, chicken, pork or beef. Researchers are warning anyone who will listen that if we do not change the way we produce meat and poultry, it is not a matter of if, but when we will run out of effective antibiotics.

Regulations Are Needed

Because overuse of antibiotics carries such serious implications for society, it makes sense to regulate them. And regulations do not need to translate into lower yields for farmers. Since the 1990s, Denmark has regulated and reduced antibiotic use in farm animals, and studies show that meat production was not adversely affected.

We are saddened by the E. coli outbreak in Europe, but we hope it revives an international discussion about antibiotic abuse. Because illnesses spread so easily through travel and trade in today's increasingly globalized world, it is important for countries to tackle this important issue together.

Policymakers need to look at ways to regulate antibiotics. Doctors and patients should exercise restraint and be judicious in their use of antibiotics. Farmers must take responsibility for the methods they use to produce larger animals. And pharmaceutical companies should continue to research promising alternatives to antibiotics.

It is time to stop the complacent overuse of antibiotics. Using them for anything other than treating infection is reckless and irresponsible.

We need to use less before they're useless.

EVALUATING THE AUTHOR'S ARGUMENTS:

According to the *Deseret News,* public health campaigns alone cannot stop the overuse of antibiotics—regulations and restrictions on the use of these medicines must be enforced. Do you agree that regulating antibiotics is an effective way to prevent their misuse? Why or why not?

A Ban on Growth-Boosting Antibiotics in Farming Is Not Justified

"There's no sense in limiting the use of antibiotics on the farm if medical misuse is not going to be curtailed."

Nevil Speer

Nevil Speer is chair of the Animal Agriculture Advocacy Council for the National Institute for Animal Agriculture. In this viewpoint Speer argues that the public interest groups have wrongly blamed the farming industry for the spread of antibiotic-resistant bacteria. There is no data connecting the use of antibiotics in farm animals to an increase in drug-resistant infections in humans, he contends. Furthermore, countries that have banned the nontherapeutic use of antibiotics in livestock have seen no decline in antibiotic resistance among people. The increase in drug-resistant infections in humans is more likely due to medical professionals who allow patients to overuse antibiotics, Speer maintains.

AS YOU READ, CONSIDER THE FOLLOWING QUESTIONS:
  1. What did Hurd et al. discover in their 2004 risk assessment focusing on the use of antibiotics in animals, according to the author?
  2. According to Speer, when did penicillin first require a doctor's prescription in the United States?
  3. As stated by the author, what happened in Denmark after that country banned the use of growth-promoting antibiotics in farm animals?

A lot of misinformation is put out to the general public about food and food production. The agriculture industry can shake off a lot of that and move forward, but if there's one issue where agriculture really takes it on the chin, it's about the use of antibiotics for livestock.

That's unfortunate, though, because the judicious use of antibiotics (or lack thereof) and the potential for antibiotic resistance are matters of public health that touch everyone in some form.

That importance underscores the necessity of having genuine, science-based discussion of the issue. Smoke and mirrors won't suffice. Nonetheless, the issue has come to the forefront in recent months.

A Lawsuit Against the FDA

First, a coalition of public interest groups filed a lawsuit charging that the Food & Drug Administration (FDA) violated federal law by failing to actively withdraw approval of penicillin and tetracycline use in animal feed for non-therapeutic, growth-promoting purposes after FDA itself suggested that use of the two drugs facilitates development of antibiotic-resistant bacterial strains. Hence, the suit is predicated on the claim of "growing evidence that the spread of bacteria immune to antibiotics has clear links to the overuse of antibiotics in the food industry."

Dovetailing that effort came proposed legislation in both the House and Senate aimed at reduced antibiotic use in animal agriculture. The bills are primarily designed to phase out non-therapeutic use of antibiotics in livestock. The talking points are the same.

For example, Sen. Dianne Feinstein (D., Cal.), upon reintroducing the legislation, said, "The rampant overuse of antibiotics in agriculture creates drug-resistant bacteria, an increasing threat to human beings. . . . The effectiveness of antibiotics for humans is jeopardized when they are used to fatten healthy pigs or speed the growth of chickens."

US secretary of agriculture Mike Johanns speaks about the use of medicines to enhance livestock growth at the National Institute for Animal Agriculture, which argues that public-interest groups have wrongly blamed the agricultural industry for the spread of antibiotic-resistant bacteria.

Some Examples of Prophylactic Uses of Antibiotics in Animals

Use		
After surgery	Before transportation	Stressful conditions
Dry-cow therapy	Potential outbreaks	

Taken from: Antimicrobial Resistance Learning Site. "Introduction to Antimicrobial Usage in Animals." Michigan State University, 2011. amrls.cvm.msu.edu/pharmacology/antimicrobial-usage-in-animals.

The Issue Is Not That Simple

So, the "logic" is that antibiotics are utilized in farm animals, resistant strains of bacteria fail to be contained and, thus, escape the farm, the public is subsequently exposed to such bacteria via various avenues (including consumption of meat), people eventually become ill and, ultimately, the illness is unresponsive to treatment.

Therefore, you see efforts to curtail ongoing use in food production settings and to pre-empt approval for new antibiotics and/or uses of existing antimicrobials in livestock. The average person hearing that type of rhetoric is going to immediately assume that the aforementioned litigation and legislation are necessary.

However, the issue isn't that simple. As I said, it's a public health issue, and the matter of resistance doesn't end simply from removing the subtherapeutic use of antibiotics in livestock production. The issue must be addressed comprehensively.

A Disservice to the Public

There has never been a scientifically documented link between antibiotic use in livestock and an increasing risk of bacterial resistance in people. Therefore, laws and lawsuits simply make agriculture a political scapegoat, and that's a disservice to the public.

In fact, to the contrary, [H. Scott] Hurd et al. (*Journal of Food Protection*, 2004) demonstrated in their farm-to-patient risk assessment that the use of antibiotics in farm animals represents a "very low risk of human treatment failure," ranging from one in 10 million to one in 3 billion.

The medical community must take part in this conversation. Antibiotic prescription practices must be addressed. Frivolous treatment has become widespread. Numerous studies reveal that patients expect antibiotics, regardless of appropriateness.

Doctors, often time-crunched and motivated to maintain their patient base, frequently acquiesce to patient pressure. Concerns about potential resistance or misuse ("saving some for later") go unaddressed in the doctor/patient relationship.

Resistance Is Not New

Lest we forget, resistance is not a new phenomenon; it was on the radar screen long before antibiotics were used regularly in livestock production.

Maryn McKenna, author of *Superbug*, explains it like this: "Penicillin (released to the public in 1944) was a wonder drug, the first glimpse of the antibiotic miracle that would quell the ancient scourge of infectious disease, and its inventors were heroes. A portrait of (Sir Alexander) Fleming appeared on the cover of *Time* in May 1944 over the caption: 'His penicillin will save more lives than war can spend.'

"It was freely sold over the counter, in mouthwash, sore-throat lozenges, first-aid ointments, even cosmetics," McKenna wrote.

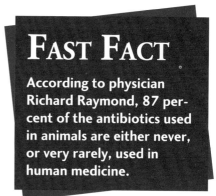

FAST FACT

According to physician Richard Raymond, 87 percent of the antibiotics used in animals are either never, or very rarely, used in human medicine.

Not until 1951 did penicillin require a doctor's prescription in the U.S. Fleming even predicted that resistance would develop, warning during his Nobel prize acceptance speech in 1945, "There is the danger that the ignorant man may easily under-dose himself and, by exposing his microbes to non-lethal quantities of the drug, make them resistant," according to McKenna.

She wrote, "Fleming was sadly right, though amidst the joy over penicillin's impact, the research that would prove his prediction received little publicity."

A New Ban Makes No Sense

A strict focus on eliminating the subtherapeutic use of antibiotics in livestock is a case of target fixation.

We can try to be like Denmark and completely eliminate the subtherapeutic use of antibiotics in livestock production, but that fails on several counts.

First, it's not effective in eliminating antibiotic use at the farm level. In the years following Denmark's ban, it was revealed that therapeutic use of antibiotics to treat animal disease increased more than 200% between 1998 and 2009. Second, there has been no documentation that antibiotic resistance in people has declined. Last, it completely overlooks the human side of the issue.

A new rule or ban doesn't automatically make everything better.

Here's our point: There's no sense in limiting the use of antibiotics on the farm if medical misuse is not going to be curtailed. The issue must be addressed comprehensively, not to mention that there has never been a scientifically documented link between antibiotic use in livestock and an increasing risk of bacterial resistance in people.

Antibiotic resistance is not a new phenomenon. As far back as December 1940, before the newly discovered drug penicillin had ever been tested in a person, scientists expressed concerns that the common gut bacteria *Escherichia coli* [*E. coli*] seemed to be evolving a defense against the new antibiotic and was producing an enzyme that kept penicillin from working. Two years later, scientists demonstrated experimentally that staph bacteria could also develop protection against the effects of penicillin.

The solution to future antibiotic use and resistance issues lies in science—not lulling the general public into a false sense of security.

Chapter 2

How Should Antibiotics Be Used?

The use of antibiotics to promote livestock growth has engendered a hot debate.

Viewpoint 1

Physicians Should Stop Prescribing Antibiotics Inappropriately

Jane E. Brody

"When an antibiotic is prescribed, it is wise to ask what the drug is and whether it is necessary."

The author of the following selection, Jane E. Brody, contends that too many physicians perpetrate the misuse of antibiotics. Brody argues that often antibiotics, particular fluoroquinolones, are inappropriately prescribed to patients. These drugs are meant for life-threatening bacterial infections, but are becoming prescribed for more mild diseases. Brody cites several cases where patients had been prescribed fluoroquinolones for relatively minor health problems, and the result was severe reactions and debilitating side effects from the antibiotics. The author urges both patients and doctors to ask whether antibiotics are necessary when evaluating an illness.

AS YOU READ, CONSIDER THE FOLLOWING QUESTIONS:
  1. What type of illnesses should the class of fluoroquinolones antibiotics be reserved for, according to the author?
  2. What are some of the documented side effects associated with the use of fluoroquinolones, as stated in the viewpoint?
  3. What questions should be asked by a patient when an antibiotic is prescribed, according to the author?

Antibiotics are important drugs, often restoring health and even saving lives. But like all drugs, they can have unwanted and serious side effects, some of which may not become apparent until many thousands of patients have been treated.

Such is the case with an important class of antibiotics known as fluoroquinolones. The best known are Cipro (ciprofloxacin), Levaquin (levofloxacin) and Avelox (moxifloxacin). In 2010, Levaquin was the best-selling antibiotic in the United States.

But by last year [2011] it was also the subject of more than 2,000 lawsuits from patients who had suffered severe reactions after taking it.

Part of the problem is that fluoroquinolones are often inappropriately prescribed. Instead of being reserved for use against serious, perhaps life-threatening bacterial infections like hospital-acquired pneumonia, these antibiotics are frequently prescribed for sinusitis, bronchitis, earaches and other ailments that may resolve on their own or can be treated with less potent drugs or nondrug remedies—or are caused by viruses, which are not susceptible to antibiotics.

In an interview, Mahyar Etminan, a pharmacological epidemiologist at the University of British Columbia, said the drugs were overused "by lazy doctors who are trying to kill a fly with an automatic weapon."

Dr. Etminan directed a study published in April [2012] in *The Journal of the American Medical Association* showing that the risk of suffering a potentially blinding retinal detachment was nearly fivefold higher among current users of fluoroquinolones, compared with nonusers. In another study submitted for publication, he documented a significantly increased risk of acute kidney failure among users of these drugs.

The conditions Dr. Etminan has studied are relatively easy to research because they result in hospitalizations with diagnoses that are computerized and tracked in databases. Far more challenging to study are the array of diffuse, confusing symptoms suffered by fluoroquinolone users like Lloyd Balch, a 33-year-old Manhattan resident and Web site manager for City College of New York.

In an interview, Mr. Balch said he was healthy until April 20, when a fever and cough prompted him to see a doctor. Nothing was heard through a stethoscope, but a chest X-ray indicated a mild case of pneumonia, and he was given Levaquin. Although he had heard of problems with Levaquin and asked the doctor if he might take a different antibiotic, he was told Levaquin was the drug he needed.

After just one dose, he developed widespread pain and weakness. He called to report this reaction, but was told to take the next dose. But the next pill, he said, "eviscerated" him, causing pain in all his joints and vision problems.

Debilitating Side Effects

In addition to being unable to walk uphill, climb stairs or see clearly, his symptoms included dry eyes, mouth and skin; ringing in his ears; delayed urination; uncontrollable shaking; burning pain in his eyes and feet; occasional tingling in his hands and feet; heart palpitations; and muscle spasms in his back and around his eyes. Though Mr. Balch's reaction is unusual, doctors who have studied the side effects of fluoroquinolones say others have suffered similar symptoms.

Three and a half months after he took that second pill, these symptoms persist, and none of the many doctors of different specialties he has consulted has been able to help. Mr. Balch is now working with a physical therapist, but in a phone consultation with Dr. David Flockhart, an expert in fluoroquinolone side effects at the Indiana University School of Medicine, he was told it could take a year for his symptoms to resolve, if they ever do disappear completely.

FAST FACT

Misuse of antibiotics jeopardizes the usefulness of essential drugs. Decreasing inappropriate antibiotic use is the best way to control resistance, according to the CDC (Centers for Disease Control and Prevention).

Guidelines by the American Thoracic Society state that fluoroquinolones should not be used as a first-line treatment for community-acquired pneumonia; it recommends that doxycycline or a macrolide be tried first. Mr. Balch didn't know this, or he might have fought harder to get a different antibiotic.

Adverse reactions to fluoroquinolones may occur almost anywhere in the body. In addition to occasional unwanted effects on the musculoskeletal, visual and renal systems, the drugs in rare cases can seriously

Sir Alexander Fleming (in portrait), who discovered penicillin, is quoted as having said regarding research on antibiotics, "One sometimes finds what one is not looking for."

injure the central nervous system (causing "brain fog," depression, hallucinations and psychotic reactions), the heart, liver, skin (painful, disfiguring rashes and phototoxicity), the gastrointestinal system (nausea and diarrhea), hearing and blood sugar metabolism.

The rising use of these potent drugs has also been blamed for increases in two very serious, hard-to-treat infections: antibiotic-resistant Staphylococcus aureus (known as MRSA) and severe diarrhea caused by Clostridium difficile. One study found that fluoroquinolones were responsible for 55 percent of C. difficile infections at one hospital in Quebec [Ontario, Canada].

Fluoroquinolones carry a "black box" warning mandated by the Food and Drug Administration [FDA] that tells doctors of the link to tendinitis and tendon rupture and, more recently, about the drugs' ability to block neuromuscular activity. But consumers don't see these highlighted alerts, and patients are rarely informed of the risks by prescribing doctors. Mr. Balch said he was never told about the black-box warnings.

Lack of Long-Term Studies

No one knows how often serious adverse reactions occur. The F.D.A.'s reporting system for adverse effects is believed to capture only about 10 percent of them. Complicating the problem is that, unlike retinal detachments that were linked only to current or very recent use of a fluoroquinolone, the drugs' adverse effects on other systems can show up weeks or months after the treatment ends; in such cases, patients' symptoms may never be associated with prior fluoroquinolone therapy.

No long-term studies have been done among former users of these antibiotics. Fibromyalgia-like symptoms have been associated with fluoroquinolones, and some experts suggest that some cases of fibromyalgia may result from treatment with a fluoroquinolone.

A half-dozen fluoroquinolones have been taken off the market because of unjustifiable risks of adverse effects. Those that remain are undeniably important drugs, when used appropriately. But doctors at the Centers for Disease Control and Prevention have expressed concern that too often fluoroquinolones are prescribed unnecessarily as a "one size fits all" remedy without considering their suitability for different patients.

Experts caution against giving these drugs to certain patients who face higher than average risks of bad reactions—children under age 18, adults over 60, and pregnant and nursing women—unless there is no effective alternative. The risk of adverse effects is also higher among people with liver disease and those taking corticosteroids or nonsteroidal anti-inflammatory drugs.

When an antibiotic is prescribed, it is wise to ask what the drug is and whether it is necessary, what side effects to be alert for, whether there are effective alternatives, when to expect the diagnosed condition to resolve, and when to call if something unexpected happens or recovery seems delayed.

At the same time, when an antibiotic is appropriately prescribed, it is extremely important to take the full prescription as directed and not to stop treatment when the patient simply begins to feel better.

Physicians Should Prescribe Antibiotics on a "Wait-and-See" Basis

"By offering the wait-and-see prescriptions, doctors can help families save time and money."

Serena Gordon

In the viewpoint that follows *Health Day* reporter Serena Gordon summarizes a Yale University study of antibiotic use in children with ear infections. The study concluded that antibiotics are not needed for most ear infections, explains Gordon. The study also found that when parents were given an antibiotic prescription for their children but were told to fill it only if symptoms grew worse, most of the children got better without antibiotics. The promotion of such "wait-and-see" prescriptions, then, is an effective way to avoid overuse of antibiotics. It can also be of great help to families, who could still fill a prescription if need be without having to revisit the doctor.

AS YOU READ, CONSIDER THE FOLLOWING QUESTIONS:

1. According to Gordon, how many antibiotic prescriptions are filled each year to treat ear infections?
2. In David Spiro's study evaluating the use of antibiotics in children with ear infections, as cited by the author, what percentage of parents given "wait-and-see" prescriptions ended up filling them?
3. As stated by David Spiro, quoted by Gordon, which children should *not* be given wait-and-see prescriptions?

Children with acute ear infections may not need antibiotics to get better, even when the infection is severe enough to prompt a visit to the emergency room.

A new study found that almost two-thirds of children given a prescription for antibiotics—just in case—didn't need to have the prescription filled to get better.

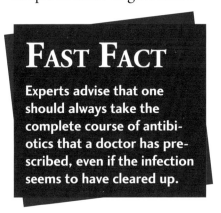

FAST FACT

Experts advise that one should always take the complete course of antibiotics that a doctor has prescribed, even if the infection seems to have cleared up.

"Our study evaluated a 'wait-and-see' prescription for ear infections in children," said the study's lead author, Dr. David Spiro, who was at Yale University School of Medicine at the time of the study. "Compared to children who were given antibiotics, children in the wait-and-see group had the same outcomes."

Empowering Families

Spiro, who now heads Pediatric Emergency Medicine at Doernbecher Children's Hospital and Oregon Health and Science University in Portland, said that by giving parents a prescription and asking them not to fill the prescription unless the child developed a higher fever or had continued ear pain, doctors can empower families to become part of the child's healthcare team.

Additionally, he said, by offering the wait-and-see prescriptions, doctors can help families save time and money. That's because if the child's condition worsens, parents don't have to take time off from work to go see the doctor again if they already have a prescription in hand.

The study findings are published in the Sept. 13 [2006] issue of the *Journal of the American Medical Association.*

Avoiding Unnecessary Antibiotics

Each year, about 15 million antibiotic prescriptions are filled to treat acute ear infections—called acute otitis media by doctors. There are several reasons why doctors would like to see this number go down.

The first is that acute otitis media often gets better on its own, with no treatment. That means children may be unnecessarily exposed to

This illustration depicts an inner-ear infection. Every year about 15 million prescriptions for antibiotics to treat acute ear infections are filled.

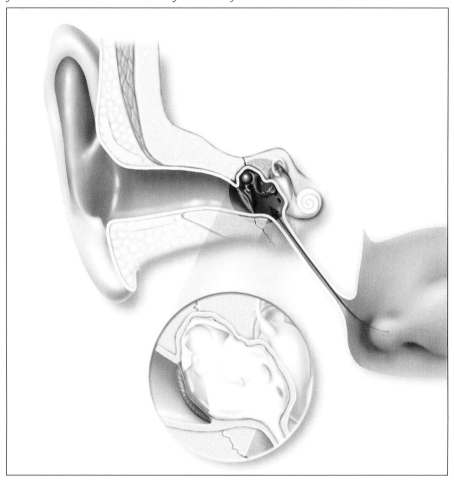

What Illnesses Actually Need Antibiotics?

Yes	No	Maybe
Strep throat (if it is confirmed with a strep test)	Cold or flu (they are viral, not bacterial, so antibiotics do not work)	Ear infection (depends on whether it is viral or bacterial)
Pneumonia	Bronchitis (likewise, it is almost always viral, not bacterial)	Vaginal infections (depends on type)
Urinary tract infection		

Taken from: Levi Brown. "Antibiotics Are Not Candy, but We Pop Them Like Skittles. . . ." *Redbook*, June 2012.

antibiotic side effects. The second reason is that there's growing concern about antibiotic resistance, and if antibiotics are given to children who really don't need them, this will just contribute to the problem.

Previous studies have looked at children who don't have severe otitis media, and those studies found that children often get better without antibiotic treatment. The new study's goal was to look at a sicker group of children and see if they could wait to take antibiotics without developing complications.

Details of the Study

Spiro and his colleagues recruited 283 children between the ages of 6 months and 12 years old who were seen in the emergency room because of an acute ear infection. All of the children were given ibuprofen and pain-relieving ear drops.

One hundred and forty-five children were randomly selected for the standard prescription group; they were given a prescription for antibiotics and told to fill it. And there were 138 children in the "wait-and-see" group. In this group, parents were still given a prescription, but they were asked to wait to fill it. The parents in this group were told to fill the prescription only if the child hadn't shown signs of improvement or had worsened in the 48 hours following their emergency-room visit.

In the standard prescription group, 87 percent of parents filled their child's prescriptions, while only 38 percent of the parents in the wait-and-see group ended up doing so. There were no statistically significant differences in the rates of fever, ear pain, and additional medical visits between the two groups.

The most common reasons that parents in the wait-and-see group ended up filling the prescriptions were fever and ear pain.

"If your child has an uncomplicated ear infection, ask your doctor if they can give you a wait-and-see prescription," Spiro suggested.

Parents Are Getting the Message

Dr. Irwin Benuck, attending pediatrician at Children's Memorial Hospital in Chicago and professor of clinical pediatrics at Northwestern University, said parents, especially younger parents, are getting the message that antibiotics aren't always the answer for every illness.

"Pediatricians are trying as hard as they can not to prescribe antibiotics unless they're necessary," he said.

Benuck said the new study confirms that antibiotics aren't needed for most ear infections, though he noted that he would have preferred if the researchers had been able to recheck the children's ears rather than rely on the parents' report that the child was better.

Spiro said there are some children who shouldn't be given a wait-and-see prescription. They include babies under 6 months of age, children with chronic ear infections, and children who appear seriously ill.

EVALUATING THE AUTHOR'S ARGUMENTS:

In this selection, Serena Gordon provides evidence that antibiotic misuse decreases when doctors offer parents a "wait-and-see" antibiotic prescription for their sick children. In the previous viewpoint, however, the author contends that physicians are to blame for antibiotic misuse because they prescribe antibiotics when they are not necessary. Given what you have read in each of these selections, do you think that wait-and-see prescriptions would prevent the overuse of antibiotics? Why or why not?

Testimony/ Recommendations to: The House Majority Policy Committee Hearing on Combating Lyme Disease

"Lyme sometimes requires more than a short course [of antibiotics] to make people better."

Patricia V. Smith

Lyme disease is an infection transmitted by the bite of ticks carrying the *Borrelia burgdorferi* bacterium. Currently the most prevalent vector-borne (carried and transmitted by another creature) disease in the United States, Lyme disease is also found in dozens of countries worldwide. In the following viewpoint, excerpted from her testimony before a Pennsylvania state legislative committee, Patricia V. Smith argues that more must be done to prevent and treat this infection. As is true for a variety of serious illnesses, Smith contends, chronic Lyme disease may require long-term courses of antibiotics. However, insurance companies often pressure doctors and patients to follow overly rigid guidelines in treating this illness. Because of concerns about antibiotic overuse and bacteria's developing resistance to medicines, Lyme patients can be denied the long-term treatment that they need, says Smith. She maintains that doctors should be allowed to prescribe long-term use of antibiotics for patients with chronic Lyme disease. Smith is president of the Lyme Disease Association, an advocacy organization.

AS YOU READ, CONSIDER THE FOLLOWING QUESTIONS:
1. According to the CDC, as cited by Smith, who is most likely to acquire Lyme disease?
2. What factors are contributing to higher tick populations and increased incidences of Lyme disease, according to the author?
3. According to Smith, what other illnesses are treated with long-term courses of antibiotics?

Thank you all for the opportunity to testify on this very important issue, Lyme disease.

As background: The Lyme Disease Association (LDA) is all-volunteer national non profit devoted to education, research funding, prevention & patient support. It has 34 allied organizations nationwide, including a PA affiliate, LDASEPA, and a PA Chapter, which primarily focuses on education. LDA is part of the 2009 Combined Federal Campaign (CFC) as a national charity. We have presented 10 fully CME accredited scientific conferences, 8 jointly sponsored by Columbia University, 3 held in Philadelphia, which is also being considered as our 2010 conference venue.

LDA's LymeAid 4 Kids fund, developed with author Amy Tan, dispenses money for children without insurance—19 Pennsylvania children have benefited to date from this fund. LDA provides research grants coast-to-coast and has funded several projects in Pennsylvania connected to researchers at Fox Chase Cancer Center, University of Pennsylvania, Edinboro University of Pennsylvania, and University of Pittsburg School of Nursing and has partnered with its CT affiliate, TFL, to endow the first center in the world at Columbia to study chronic Lyme in 2007. That same year, I was invited to speak at Ft. Collins, Colorado, to the Centers for Disease

Control & Prevention's (CDC) Vector-Borne Diseases Division where Lyme is studied.

LDA is an Environmental Protection Agency (EPA) PESP partner and sits on a working group with EPA and with CDC. We are currently developing measures to help reduce children's exposure to Lyme disease. We hope to use existing tools such as the LDA website which is also linked with EPA's site, to provide parents with educational materials to complement an EPA-funded prevention video and an interactive video game for kids being developed by NJ Medical School in collaboration with LDA. The parent materials may contain links to composition/effectivity of pesticides and property management techniques for schools. We are also seeking to publish with the National Association of School Nurses, possibly using existing publications to publish the prevention message to schools.

> ## FAST FACT
>
> Since 1975, when it was first identified in cases in Lyme and Old Lyme, Connecticut, at least five hundred thousand Americans have contracted Lyme disease.

A CDC study of New Jersey children K–12 with Lyme showed the median number of missed school days was 140; median duration of home instruction, 153 days; 78% of parents said their children experienced a fall in grade point average during illness; 79% experienced a decrease in friends; ". . . isolated from social groups and missing out on cultural, sports and social activities. . . . School performance of nearly all patients fell sometimes drastically, and in several instances, was said to interfere with selection by colleges and universities."[i] A study at Columbia demonstrated a drop of 22 IQ points in a student with Lyme disease, later reversed with treatment.[ii]

According to CDC, boys & girls ages 5–9 are at the greatest risk of acquiring Lyme,[iii] the most prevalent vector-borne disease in the US today, reported in all 50 states. From 1990 through 2008, PA ranked #2 nationwide with 51,266 reported Lyme cases. CDC states only 10% of cases that meet CDC surveillance criteria are reported,[iv] meaning over 1/2 million (512,660) PA residents developed Lyme that met the surveillance criteria over that time, a number that includes my now late parents.

That number is only a fraction of cases that probably occurred, since CDC's surveillance criteria are meant for comparing cases of Lyme in one state to another and don't include cases clinically diagnosed by physicians—meaning cases without an EM rash or without a positive test. Numbers in PA are sharply rising, with 2009 numbers already more than double 2008 total numbers (7,540/3602).

The situation isn't likely to improve soon. Deforestation, increase in deer herds and climate changes are said to be contributing to increased tick populations and expanded tick ranges, increasing disease burden. According to Penn State College of Agricultural Sciences, a 1960's survey in PA identified 20 tick species in-state, with deer ticks found only in Philadelphia County. Furthermore, in the late 80s, deer ticks were mostly limited to the southeast corner, the north central region around Elk State Forest and the Presque Isle peninsula in Erie but now they are established in more areas around the state and 25 species have been identified.

Ninety percent of tick identification submissions to Penn State consist of 4 ticks, 3 of which transmit many tick-borne diseases to humans:

1) American dog tick (RMSF, tularemia, ehrlichiosis, tick paralysis);
2) blacklegged tick [deer tick] (Lyme, babesiosis, anaplasmosis, Powassan encephalitis, tick paralysis, tularemia, bartonellosis); and
3) lone star tick (ehrlichiosis, tularemia, RMSF, tick paralysis, Q fever, and STARI). Southern Tick-Associated rash illness (STARI), looks and acts like Lyme, sometimes has the same bull's eye rash, is treated the same way, but there is no test for it. The lone star tick is much more aggressive than a deer tick and will stalk you from 50 feet away. Tick-borne diseases are increasing in general, but Lyme itself increased 250% nationwide from 1993 through 2008.

Lyme is now found in 65 countries worldwide. A UN commissioned study indicates ticks in Sweden have moved almost as far north as the Arctic Circle and are being found in January. Reports from researchers and patients seem to confirm that latter finding in the Northeast. In January 2005, my daughter pulled a fully engorged deer tick off my then 5-year old granddaughter's ear. It was 25°.

Two items greatly influence the ability and willingness of doctors to diagnosis and treat Lyme patients, including children—the first is the CDC surveillance criteria. Despite CDC's warning that the surveillance criteria are NOT intended for diagnosis, treatment, or insurance reimbursement, but are only intended for disease surveillance reporting, most doctors are inappropriately using them to diagnose and treat and insurance companies are using them to deny treatment reimbursement. The CDC criteria for an endemic region are: an EM rash (plus a required test in a non-endemic region), OR major system involvement plus positive blood work.

Although CDC criteria are for surveillance purposes only, patients who do not meet that criteria must scramble to find physicians willing to risk making a clinical diagnosis for Lyme disease, one based on symptoms, history, ruling out other diseases, one which does not require a positive test for diagnosis. Problems about diagnosis are fueled by unreliable Lyme testing that is 40–60% accurate,[v] and by the fact that less than 50% of people develop the classic bull's eye rash.[vi]

The second item influencing doctors' ability and willingness to treat is the Infectious Diseases Society of America (IDSA) Lyme treatment guidelines ("Guidelines"). They recommend against any long-term treatment for chronic Lyme; against entire classes of antibiotics; against alternative treatments; against some supplements; and against individual physician discretion in diagnosis and treatment. IDSA says there is NO chronic Lyme disease.

Despite a disclaimer that says they are NOT mandatory, actual experiences demonstrate the Guidelines have become de facto law. Medical boards, health departments, hospitals, insurers, schools, pharmacists, and IDSA doctors themselves often hold that position, leading to doctor prosecution and inability of patients to get medical care for Lyme disease. The abuse has been so blatant that Connecticut State Attorney General Richard Blumenthal initiated an investigation of the IDSA Guidelines' development process.

In a 2008 settlement Agreement with IDSA, Mr. Blumenthal stated: "This agreement vindicates my investigation—finding undisclosed financial interests . . . held by several of the most powerful IDSA panelists. The . . . panel improperly ignored or minimized consideration of alternative medical opinion and evidence regarding chronic Lyme disease, potentially raising serious questions about whether the

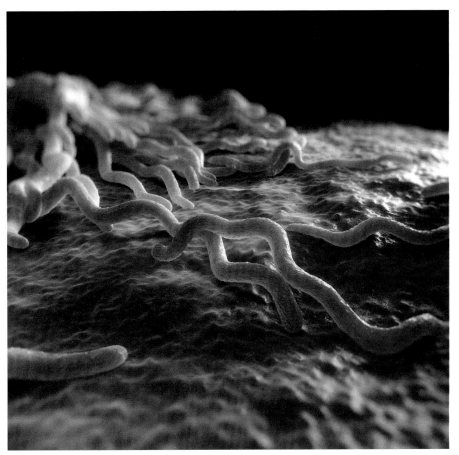

The author argues that Lyme disease, caused by the bacterium Borrelial burgdorferi (shown), may require long-term antibiotic treatment.

recommendations reflected all relevant science . . . The IDSA's Lyme guideline process lacked important procedural safeguards. . . ."[vii] IDSA had to form a new panel, which heard testimony in July 2009, re-looking at the guidelines, but it again excluded chronic Lyme treating doctors as panel members.

There are other Lyme treatment guidelines which differ from IDSA's, which do allow doctor discretion in diagnosis and treatment, and do recognize that Lyme sometimes requires more than a short course to make people better. They provide the basis for a second standard of care for Lyme disease. Published by the International Lyme & Associated Diseases Society (ILADS), a professional medical and research organization,[viii] they're ignored by IDSA and often not disclosed as an option by doctors to patients. They are published on

Reported Cases of Lyme Disease in Some Eastern States

State	Year		
	1995	2002	2009
Connecticut	1,548	4,631	2,751
Massachusetts	189	1,807	4,019
New Jersey	1,703	2,349	4,598
New York	4,438	5,535	4,134
Pennsylvania	1,562	3,989	4,950

Taken from: Centers for Disease Control and Prevention. "Reported Cases of Lyme Disease by State or Locality." 2010. www.cdc.gov.

the Department of Health and Human Services National Guidelines Clearing House website, recognizing them as being evidenced-based.[ix]

ILADS' approach recognizes that patients who are not diagnosed quickly or not treated appropriately can become chronically ill—one study shows that Lyme patients suffer a degree of disability equal to that of patients with congestive heart failure.[x] Yet many of these patients, often multi-members of one family,[xi] now have to travel many hours outside Pennsylvania to find care for their Lyme. They don't have the resources nor the health to fight the vested interests stacked against them, which is why legislation is often necessary to protect doctors who treat, ensuring that in-state treating doctors cannot be prosecuted for unprofessional conduct solely for providing long-term treatment based on clinical judgment. Rhode Island, Connecticut and California have passed protective legislation. Massachusetts, Minnesota, and Pennsylvania have introduced it, with another state about to do so.

Despite two standards of care for Lyme, physicians continue to be monitored by insurance companies who say stop prescribing antibiotics for Lyme disease or leave the insurance plan. Some doctors then leave the plan voluntarily, others are forced out. Some continue treating patients without accepting insurance. Other physicians fear scrutiny from the insurance companies and stop treating Lyme disease entirely, leading to a scarcity of physicians.

Patients lack of insurance coverage leads to limited courses of antibiotics, often not effective in eradicating the Lyme bacterium, which has the ability to hide inside cells, kill human lymphocytes and certain B cells and to change into other forms. Legislation requiring insurance companies to cover patients for Lyme treatment has been passed in Rhode Island and Connecticut and has been introduced in Pennsylvania. The legislature should pass Pennsylvania Lyme bills HB 894 & SB346 which provide for doctor protection, insurance coverage, and creation of a task force.

Most of the opposition to Lyme doctor protection legislation comes from the IDSA itself. You have heard how doctors who don't follow IDSA Guidelines but use their own clinical skills to diagnose and treat face medical board discipline, hospital privilege/post revocation, and insurance plan exclusion if they do not march lockstep with IDSA, creating a "chilled" treatment climate.

IDSA sometimes cites development of antibiotic resistance for opposing legislation, despite resistance most often developing due to under usage rather than over usage of antibiotics. The Union of Concerned Scientists feels a significant cause of resistant bacteria may be an estimated 70% of antibiotics in the U.S. being fed to healthy pigs, cows, and chickens to promote growth and prevent disease.[xii] Antibiotic resistant strains often spread due to improper hygiene by medical personnel in hospitals. IDSA also ignores the fact that other diseases are allowed long-term treatment with antibiotics including tuberculosis, Q fever endocarditis, and even acne. Terribly sick Lyme patients are singled out to be left without treatment because of undocumented accusations of resistance due to treating sick people.

IDSA even opposes federal legislation (HR 1179 C. Smith [NJ] 86 co-sponsors, S 1352 C. Dodd [CT] 8 co-sponsors), Lyme & Tick-Borne diseases Prevention, Research and Education Act 2009, which provides much needed research funds—$100M over 5 years, particularly for an accurate test to help resolve many Lyme-related issues. IDSA indicates they do not like the constitution of a Lyme and tick-borne diseases federal advisory committee created by the bills because it contains patient and treating physician reps with different viewpoints, although many other diseases have that type of panel.

Following IDSA Guidelines can lead to delayed diagnosis and treatment. According to an actuarial study on Lyme costs, "37% of the financial costs of this disease is incurred before the correct diagnosis is made."[xiii] A delay in diagnosis also leads to more chronic disease since the Lyme bacterium can get into the brain within 24 hours of a tick bite.[xiv] Chronic Lyme is more costly to patients physically, mentally, and financially. According to a 1998 CDC journal study, early Lyme costs* averaged $161 per patient and neurologic longstanding Lyme disease averaged $61,243.[xv] Chronic Lyme is also more costly to the state and federal government in terms of disability and education e.g., special services, home instruction, substitute teachers.[xvi] Allowing doctor discretion in diagnosing and treating can cut costs and most importantly, human suffering.

In 2009 LDA and its partner groups were successful in having language included in the US House Appropriations bill which passed the full House and includes the terms "chronic Lyme disease" and "persistence." The language also passed the Senate Committee and is awaiting full Senate vote. Full passage will help Lyme patients receive the medical treatment they require.

Besides legislation, public and physician education is very important. LDA just received a copy of a letter from a western PA physician to his patient. The patient was bitten by something and had a possible bull's eye rash. The doctor was unsure if Lyme was even in the county, checked with health department officials who said the reported cases there were not from within the county, although how that was determined is not stated. He thus determined Lyme was probably not endemic there. The doctor requested supporting info from the patient about Lyme in the area, although he did prescribe a minimal dose of medication. A quick check by me of the canine cases in that county reported by an IDEXX Veterinary Labs survey, an LDA corporate partner, shows 122 Lyme cases there in dogs, which are sentinels for the disease.

To help states educate and combat against tick-borne diseases, LDA has developed a table of general recommendations for states:

	LDA Recommendations Table*	
WHO Implements	WHAT Is Implemented	WHY It Is Recommended
DOH	Letter sent to all licensed physicians in the state explaining the CDC surveillance criteria & alerting them that CDC criteria are not diagnostic criteria & Lyme is a mandatory reportable disease.	CDC says diagnosing is misuse of surveillance criteria. It contributes to late/improper diagnosis/delayed treatment.
Family Services Agency	Send letter to all employees cautioning them not to use Munchausen's by proxy label for parents just because they are having children treated for Lyme by licensed physician under ILADS standard of care (long-term treatment).	There are currently two standards of care and long-term treatment is acceptable under the ILADS standard of care.
Parks/public lands	Post parks alerting to presence of ticks, avoidance, removal.	Prevention
DOH	Require continuing medical education (CME) credits for state-licensed physicians including diagnosis and treatment from both standards of care. Alert physicians to available conferences, posted on DOH websites, & use electronic mail for staff members at hospitals to communicate with physicians about such events.	Lack of physician knowledge
DOH	Develop a reporting system that accepts physician diagnosed causes that do not meet the CDC criteria. Since mandatory reporting is in effect, data is already at health department and could be logged at a tier only for state purposes.	Better surveillance for Lyme disease. Can determine true diagnosed-incidence and concentrate resources in specific areas as needed.
State Department of Insurance	Alert insurers licensed in the state that they cannot deny coverage for Lyme treatment based on the CDC surveillance criteria. Alert that 2 standards of care exist, IDSA & ILADS.	Insurers using CDC criteria to deny reimbursement. Also using IDSA guidelines as de facto law.
DOE/DOH	Encourage schools to keep properties maintained, post tick warnings, and develop trip policies reflecting high risk areas.	Prevention
DOE	Encourage schools in endemic areas to provide educational forums on Lyme disease for staff and students.	Prevention and funding considerations.
DOH	Use country/local health boards to distribute information on prevention to recreation programs, camps, etc.	Local departments have closer ties to communities and understand their needs.
Medical Licensing Board	Send letters to reviewers alerting them to the fact that there are two standards of care for Lyme disease. Place physicians who treat under the ILADS standard of care on review board or place them on the "expert" referral list if such a list is used when cases against long-term treating physicians arise.	To prevent physicians from being charged w/ malpractice solely for treating Lyme long-term. If reported (often by ins. co. or other doctors who don't treat), doctors need experts free of specialty bias reviewing their charts.
Game Commission	Oversees hunting & fishing licenses—issue advisories to sportsmen, especially in the area of prevention, tick removal. Courses for hunters should include prevention materials.	High risk groups
All agencies	Work with Lyme organizations that often provide resources and fully accredited medical conferences for physicians. Apply for grants in partnership with these organizations.	Shared resources. Grantors often consider dual applicants a plus.
Police, Emergency	Add prevention materials to their training requirements.	High risk groups

On Thanksgiving at my home last week, 4 of the 12 adults had been diagnosed with Lyme disease, 2 from NJ, 2 from PA. Another from PA will probably be diagnosed with Lyme and/or another tick-borne disease called anaplasmosis. All states need to take actions to prevent the further spread of Lyme and other tick-borne diseases which are devastating entire families and to help those already infected. No one is safe from these complicated infections.

Thank you.

i David Dennis, CDC, presented study in Wall Township, NJ, October 1992, Congressional meeting. Later pub. *Lyme Times Children's Educational Issue,* ed. CALDA, Summer 2006.

ii Brian Fallon MD, *The Underdiagnosis of Neuropsychiatric Lyme Disease in Children & Adult,* The Psychiatric Clinics of North America, Vol. 21, No. 3, Sept. 1998.

iii Centers for Disease Control & Prevention, *Average Annual Incidence of Reported Cases of Lyme Disease by Age Group & Sex,* http://www.cdc.gov/ncidod/dvbid/lyme/ld_Mean AnnualIncidence.htm.

iv Paul Meade, CDC, *Herald News* 5-4-04, Jessica Adler.

v P. Coulter et al, J. Clin Microbiol. 2005 Oct.; 43(10): 5080-4 *Two Year Evaluation of Borrelia burgdorferi Culture and Supplemental Tests for Definitive Diagnosis of Lyme Disease. Lancet 1990, Journal of Clinical Investigation 1994 & S. Schutzer et al, JAMA Vol. 282, No. 20 Borrelia Burgdorferi:Specific Immune Complexes in Acute Lyme Disease, Nov. 24, '99*

vi R. Smith et al, Annals of Internal Medicine 2002; 421: 421-428, 477-479; A. Pachner, Reviews of Infectious Diseases—Vol. II, supplement 6—September–October 1989 Neurologic Manifestations of Lyme Disease, the new "Great Imitator"; J.M. Johnson, Ph.D., Chief, Public Health, NPS Ticks and Disease.

vii Office of the Connecticut Attorney General, press release, May 1, 2008.

viii Daniel Cameron, et al, Expert Review of Anti-infective therapy 2(1) Suppl. 2004.

ix AHRQ, http://www.guideline.gov/.

x Connecticut Agricultural Experiment Station, "Summary of Tick Testing Results for 2003." www.caes.state.ct.us.

xi CDC unpub. study data presented in Congressional forum, Wall NJ Oct 1992 (Later pub. in Lyme Times).

xii http://www.ucsusa.org/food_and_environment/antibiotics_and_food/myths-and-realities.

xiii Irwin Vanderhoof, *Lyme Disease the Cost to Society,* Contingencies January/Februray 1993.

xiv Steere, Allen, Mandel, Douglas, and Bennett's *Principals & Practices of Infectious Diseases,* 4th ed. 1995. xiv Martin I. Meltzer *The Cost Effectiveness of Vaccinating against Lyme Disease CDC Emerging Infectious Diseases;* Vol.5, No.3; 1999 May–June; 5(3)321-8. * This is in 1996 costs not adjusted. The following additional significant costs to society aren't measured by this table: special education needs for children, disability, increased medical and insurance costs, and livestock losses, etc. Also, there are personal loses: friends, employment, self, esteem, domicile, and breakup of families.

xv Martin I. Meltzer *The Cost Effectiveness of Vaccinating against Lyme Disease CDC Emerging Infectious Diseases;* Vol.5, No.3; 1999 May–June; 5(3)321-8. * This is 1996 costs not adjusted to 2007. The following additional costs to society aren't measured by this table: special education needs for children, disability, increased medical and insurance costs, and livestock losses, etc. Also, there are personal loses: friends, employment, self, esteem, domicile, and breakup of families.

xvi Patricia Smith, Wall Township, NJ, Board of Education member *NJ School District Study on Impact of Lyme Disease on School Districts* presented in Washington DC Congressionally hosted meeting with CDC & NIH, March 12, 1992.

* LDA recommends that State agencies consult with patient groups within state and/or the national LDA to provide input into these areas since these groups can often provide a perspective the State does otherwise not have access to, and they can provide feedback from solutions other states may have attempted/implemented. ©Lyme Disease Association, Inc. 2005 www.LymeDiseaseAssociation.org PO Box 1438 Jackson, NJ 08527 888 366 6611

In this viewpoint Patricia V. Smith maintains that Lyme
disease patients are frequently denied the treatment that
they may need—long-term courses of antibiotics—due
to concerns about antibiotic resistance. In her view, who
and what are really to blame for the increase in resistant
bacteria? Do you agree with her argument that insurance
companies and professional boards wrongly pressure doctors to avoid treating Lyme disease? Why or why not?

Hearing on Global Challenges in Diagnosing and Managing Lyme Disease

"Long-term antibiotic therapy will do patients more harm than good."

Infectious Diseases Society of America

The Infectious Diseases Society of America (IDSA) is a group representing physicians, scientists, and other health care professionals who specialize in infectious diseases. In the following viewpoint the IDSA maintains that Lyme disease should not be treated with long-term courses of antibiotics. The IDSA acknowledges that some patients have recurring symptoms long after their initial therapy for Lyme disease but that there is no evidence that these symptoms constitute a chronic form of the illness that can be cured with long-term use of antibiotics. Taking antibiotics for months or years promotes drug-resistant infections and can be deadly, asserts the IDSA.

AS YOU READ, CONSIDER THE FOLLOWING QUESTIONS:
1. By what percentage did US Lyme disease cases decrease from 2009 to 2010, as stated by the author?
2. According to the IDSA, what is the standard antibiotic treatment for Lyme disease?
3. What is "chronic" Lyme disease, according to the author?

D uring 2006–2009, the total number of Lyme disease cases reported to the Centers for Disease Control and Prevention (CDC) increased each year, albeit with no consistent trend across states. In 2010, however, confirmed cases decreased 25% and probable cases decreased 11% as compared with 2009. In addition, regional trends were apparent. Among 12 high-incidence states in the Northeastern and mid-Atlantic regions, all but Virginia reported a decrease in confirmed cases. Conversely, the number of confirmed cases increased [by more than] 20% in Minnesota and Wisconsin. The reasons for these patterns are unknown. Given the observed regional consistencies, surveillance artifact is an unlikely explanation. (MMWR, Vol. 59, No. 53, June 1, 2012, page 15)

The risk of acquiring Lyme disease for people who live in endemic areas can be lessened by taking simple, preventative steps such as avoiding brushy areas when walking in wooded areas; wearing long pants, long-sleeved shirts; using insect repellents; and thoroughly checking for ticks after being outdoors. IDSA supports efforts to further educate the public about these prevention efforts.

Another strategy worthy of discussion is a vaccine for prevention of Lyme disease. As you may know, in 1998, a Lyme disease vaccine for humans was introduced and initially was popular. Unfortunately, vaccine opponents began making unsubstantiated claims about the vaccine's side effects. These claims were not backed up by clinical data. The trials had not shown such side effects. The Food and Drug Administration (FDA) and the CDC looked into the claims, and then continued to recommend that people in or around tick-infested areas get the vaccine. However, the damage to the vaccine's public image caused vaccine sales to plummet. SmithKline Beecham, the company that manufactured the vaccine, pulled it from the market. A second Lyme disease vaccine-maker, Pasteur Merieux Connaught, perhaps because of the SmithKline Beecham experience, subsequently decided not to market its own product. Lyme vaccines remain available for animals, but not humans. IDSA would be happy to participate in discussions with Congress, the Administration, and industry to determine if a Lyme disease vaccine would be a useful tool in preventing Lyme disease and, if so, how to ensure that a safe and effective vaccine reaches recommended populations.

The National Institute for Allergy and Infectious Disease (NIAID) at the National Institutes of Health (NIH) also is finding grants for research and development of a bait vaccine to immunize wildlife in Lyme-infested areas. This effort has the potential to reduce the transmission of Lyme disease by reducing the number of ticks capable of infecting humans. Although this product is still being tested, initial data are very promising. While not a foolproof solution this effort could be combined with other prevention strategies to strengthen our defenses against Lyme disease. IDSA urges further support to continue this research.

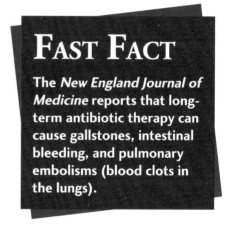

FAST FACT

The *New England Journal of Medicine* reports that long-term antibiotic therapy can cause gallstones, intestinal bleeding, and pulmonary embolisms (blood clots in the lungs).

New Diagnostics

IDSA believes that specific and more sensitive diagnostic tests for Lyme disease are needed. NIAID devotes about 20 percent of its funding for Lyme disease to research that relates directly or indirectly to diagnosis. Because of enormous advances in bioinformatics and molecular genetics, significant progress has been made in the development of new diagnostic tests. However, it must be noted that whenever any new diagnostic test is developed, it must be compared to existing diagnostic methods to ensure that it is indeed superior with respect to specificity and sensitivity before it can be widely used and applied.

Studies performed at different institutions may use a variety of experimental methods that make it impossible to compare results in a meaningful way. This is why IDSA strongly advocated for the establishment of a Serum Reference Repository with a computerized data base to accelerate the decision making process by applying uniform standards to a large number of patient cases. The NIH and CDC initiated this repository in 2008 and, at the end of 2011, began making Lyme disease and related serum samples for testing and comparison of new and current diagnostic tests with a common serum sample set for standardization available to the scientific community on a broad basis. The repository now can enable comparison of results of newly developed and existing diagnostic tests under identical conditions using the same panel of well-characterized existing diagnostic tests under identical conditions using the same panel of well-characterized reference specimens. Though the effort is still quite new, IDSA believes it has the potential to yield positive results in the development of new diagnostic tools for Lyme disease.

Post-Treatment Lyme Disease Syndrome

IDSA recognizes that Lyme disease can be painful and that the disease is not always properly identified or treated. The Society advocates for educational efforts and, as mentioned in the section above, development of improved diagnostics that will enable clinicians to accurately identify patients infected with *Borrelia burgdorferi* so appropriate treatment can be prescribed. We recognize that some patients may continue to experience prolonged Lyme disease symptoms even after a course of antibiotic therapy has killed the Lyme disease bacterium. We sympathize with these patients' suffering, but remain concerned that a diagnosis of so-called "chronic Lyme disease," suggesting that active infection is ongoing, is not supported by scientific evidence and, more alarmingly, the treatment of long-term antibiotic therapy will do patients more harm than good.

There is no scientifically accepted case definition for "chronic Lyme disease." Standard courses of antibiotics (between 10–28

Recommended Oral Antibiotic Treatment for Lyme Disease

Drug	Adult Dosage	Child Dosage
Amoxicillin	500 milligrams 3 times a day	500 milligrams per kilogram per day in 3 divided doses
Doxycycline	100 milligrams 2 times a day	4 milligrams per kilogram per day in 2 divided doses
Cefuroxime axetil	500 milligrams 2 times a day	30 milligrams per kilogram per day in 2 divided doses

Taken from: Infectious Diseases Society of America. "The Clinical Assessment, Treatment, and Prevention of Lyme Disease, Human Granulocytic Anaplasmosis, and Babesiosis: Clinical Practice Guidelines," 2013. http://cid.oxfordjournals.org/content/43/9/1089/F6.expansion.html.

days depending on the manifestation of Lyme disease) have been proven effective to clear the infection in the vast majority of cases. IDSA recognizes that some patients continue to experience Lyme symptoms, such as arthritis, after the infection has been cleared by standard antibiotic therapy. According to peer-reviewed studies, these stubborn symptoms may be due to persisting inflammatory responses, by genetically predisposed individuals, to bacterial debris left in the body after the infection is cleared as well as joint damage caused by the initial infection. One study focusing on patients with antibiotic-refractory late Lyme arthritis, published in the *Annals of Internal Medicine*, found that these symptoms may persist for nine years, but the incidence and severity of these symptoms do decrease over time and eventually stop. During the first year following the first onset of illness, 90% of patients had bouts of arthritis, and the number of individuals who continued to have recurrences decreased by 10–20% each year. (Steere, A.C. *et al. Ann.Intern. Med.*107, 725-731 [1987]).

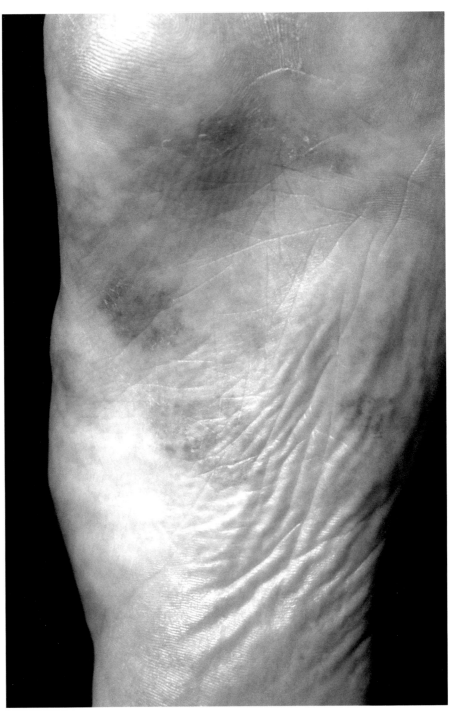

Most cases of Lyme disease, such as this one, are successfully treated with from ten to twenty-eight days of antibiotics. Some scientists argue that longer use can be dangerous due to potentially fatal complications and can promote the development of drug-resistant microbes.

Long-Term Antibiotic Therapy

Most cases of Lyme disease are successfully treated with 10–28 days of antibiotics. Using antibiotics for a very long time (months or years) does not offer superior results and can be dangerous, because it can cause potentially fatal complications and can promote the development of drug-resistant infections. Whether long-term antibiotics benefit patients with persistent symptoms of fatigue, musculoskeletal pains and neurocognitive dysfunction has been scrutinized using the highest level of scientific evidence: four placebo-controlled randomized trials do not support the use of long-term antibiotics as an appropriate treatment for Lyme disease. Though some patients report feeling better after this treatment, these results are largely anecdotal and study after study has failed to demonstrate any benefit of long-term antibiotic treatment over placebo. It should be noted that these randomized clinical studies reflected that approximately one-third of patients benefit from placebo. (Klempner MS, Hu LT, Evans J, et al. Two controlled trails of antibiotic treatment in patients with persistent symptoms and a history of Lyme disease. *N Engl J Med* 2001; 345:85-92.) (Krupp LB, Hyman LG, Grimson R. et al. Study and treatment of post Lyme disease (stop-LD): a randomized double-masked clinical trial. *Neurology* 2003; 60: 1923-30.) (Fallon BA, Sackheim HA, Keilp J, et al. Double-blind placebo-controlled retreatment with IV ceftriaxone for Lyme encephalopathy: clinical outcome [abstract 196]. In: Program and abstracts of the 10th International Conference on Lyme Borreliosis and Other Tick-Borne Diseases (Vienna, Austria). Austrian Society for Hygiene, Microbiology and Preventive Medicine. 2005. p. 116.) Hence, it is perhaps understandable why some patients and practitioners might mistakenly endorse long-term antibiotic therapy as helpful. This is precisely why it is important to perform well-designed clinical trials to distinguish if a therapeutic intervention has actual, beneficial effect in contrast to a resolution of symptoms which might merely happen on its own accord.

Further, no reliable evidence exists that supports the designation of Lyme disease as a chronic, actively infectious disease requiring ongoing antibiotic therapy. Two recent reviews—one published in the *New England Journal of Medicine* (*N Engl J Med* 357:14; October 4, 2007)* and the other in the *American Journal of Medicine* (2008) 121,

562-564—give evidence-based assessments of Lyme disease diagnoses and the recommended treatments that substantiate IDSA's position. Neither the diagnosis of so-called "chronic" Lyme disease, nor long-term antibiotic therapy are supported by the NIH CDC, American Academy of Neurology, the American College of Physicians, and the American Academy of Pediatrics, or by an overwhelming majority of experts in the field of infectious diseases medicine in this country and abroad.

Specific to the issue of global aspects of Lyme disease, although the pathogen that causes Lyme disease in Europe is somewhat different from the one we face in the U.S., eliciting more neurological symptoms rather than the primarily arthritic symptoms Americans suffer, the same short-term course of antibiotics has been proven effective in clearing Lyme disease infections in Europe. It should be noted that the IDSA's recommendations for the treatment of Lyme disease are in agreement with those of the European Federation of Neurological Societies, the European Union of Concerted Action on Lyme Borreliosis, the Canadian Public Health Network, and the German Society for Hygiene and Microbiology. They also are in agreement with recommendations made by expert panels from 10 European countries, including the Czech Republic, Denmark, Finland, France, the Netherlands, Norway, Poland, Slovenia, Sweden, and Switzerland.

IDSA recognizes that medicine is continually evolving, and the Society's members do not claim to have all the answers. Given that long term antibiotic therapy has not been found to effectively treat symptoms that persist after the initial infection is cleared, IDSA supports additional research to determine safe and effective treatments for patients that experience such long-term symptoms. IDSA will continue to periodically review its Lyme disease guidelines and update them as needed to reflect the best available scientific literature.

Conclusion

Once again, IDSA thanks Chairman Smith and Members of the Subcommittee for their attention to this issue and their interest in IDSA's perspective. The Society looks forward to working with you on matters of importance to global health.

Chapter 3

What Should Be Done to Stop the Spread of Drug-Resistant Bacteria?

A microbiologist holds a culture of antibiotic-resistant bacteria. Overuse of antibiotics is often blamed for the rise of such bacteria.

Viewpoint

1

We Can Beat Superbugs with Better Stewardship of Antibiotics

"Rather than patients asking for a prescription, we need them to ask 'do I really need antibiotics for this?'"

Trent Yarwood

Curbing antibiotic resistance will require improved supervision of antibiotic use, argues Trent Yarwood in the following viewpoint. As he explains, overuse of antibiotics is the main reason for the recent increase in drug-resistant superbugs. Too often, patients request antibiotics when they do not need them, and too many physicians do not follow the prescription guidelines for antibiotics. The author maintains that antibiotic resistance should be seen as a serious public health issue, with educational campaigns that teach patients to limit their use of antibiotics and programs that urge doctors to restrict their antibiotic prescriptions. Yarwood is an infectious diseases physician at Queensland Health and an associate lecturer at the University of Queensland in Australia.

AS YOU READ, CONSIDER THE FOLLOWING QUESTIONS:
  1. What is "antibiotic armageddon," according to the author?
  2. According to Yarwood, what percentage of antibiotic prescriptions are in keeping with the guidelines that have been set up for these medicines?
  3. As stated in the viewpoint, what percentage of patients seeing a general practitioner for a viral infection expect an antibiotic prescription?

Antibiotic resistant bacteria are becoming a major problem. Calls to action on increasing rates of resistance have been made by the World Health Organization, the US Centers for Disease Control (CDC), and by the Australian Societies for Infectious Diseases (ASID) and the Australian Society for Antimicrobials (ASA).

And the media regularly features articles about superbugs and mega-superbugs. So why, if everyone is aware of the problem, are we still not winning the fight?

Drivers of Resistance

Antibiotic resistance is caused by excessive antibiotic use. If bacteria aren't exposed to antibiotics, there's no impetus for them to become resistant. But much modern medicine would be impossible without antibiotics (most surgery, for instance) so they are a necessary "evil".

More than 80% of antibiotics are prescribed in general practice, and much of this is for upper respiratory tract infections (such as colds). These are mostly caused by viruses and almost never need antibiotics.

Patients treated with antibiotics are almost three times more likely to experience a side effect (mainly nausea), for no benefit because antibiotics won't affect the duration of their illness. And resistance can develop even after a short course of antibiotics.

Hospital patients are usually sicker than patients who visit a GP. Sometimes, they're very sick and need urgent treatment. In severe infections, the time delay until antibiotics are given is a major risk for mortality.

Since antibiotic resistance is now a fact of life in hospitals around the world, it's understandable that doctors want to give their patients the best treatment available. This can lead to "antibiotic armageddon" where the biggest, most broad-spectrum antibiotic is felt to be the best way to proceed.

Australia has excellent prescribing guidelines that are easily available for doctors to refer to when prescribing antibiotics. In practice, though, studies in Australia and elsewhere show fairly consistently that only between half and three-quarters of antibiotic prescriptions are in keeping with such guidelines.

I performed an audit of antibiotics prescribed to in-patents of a hospital I worked at. It was based on a review of their medication charts and comparison with Australian Therapeutic Guidelines. This is what I found:

- dosing errors—13%;
- choice of drug different from guidelines—11%;
- unnecessarily prolonged treatment—8% and;
- antibiotics not required at all—8%.

The Three "Es"

The solution can be simplified into three "Es"—education, expectations, and enforcement.

As medicine becomes more complex, it's increasingly difficult to teach junior doctors everything they "must know" in order to practice. Education on good prescribing habits and the importance of rational antibiotic use are critical when doctors are in the formative stage of their careers.

Doctors' expectations are also important. Not every fever requires antibiotics and broader-spectrum isn't always better are the key messages to teach.

Although there are many campaigns aimed at the public about antibiotics for colds, around half of patients seeing a GP still expect

> **FAST FACT**
>
> Bacterial diseases that have become resistant to one or more antibiotic drugs include: gonorrhea, tuberculosis, typhoid fever, meningitis, and group B strep infections.

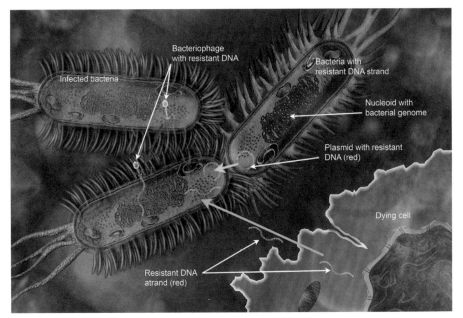

This graphic shows the three ways superbugs become resistant to antibiotics: (above left) contact with bacteria already infected by a virus with resistant DNA, (above right) already having resistant DNA, and (lower right) obtaining resistant DNA from a dying cell.

such a prescription. And although only half expect it, 73% receive one. Those who don't are twice as likely to present for another consultation.

There are two factors at play here—patients' expectation of a prescription and general practitioners' understanding of what patients expect. More worrying still is that doctors think that their prescribing doesn't impact resistance.

The result is a tragedy of the commons—patients may be aware of the risks of antibiotics in general, but feel the benefit for them outweighs the risks to the community, as superbugs only happen to someone else. In fact, the opposite is true—for viral infections patients receive no benefit from antibiotics but all of the risk.

In addition to education, a well-designed antibiotic stewardship program can significantly improve antibiotic use in hospitals. As well as improving care quality, these programs can also reduce costs and decrease length of stay in hospital and the rates of hospital-acquired infection.

Although doctors often bristle at restrictions on their practice, acceptance of these programs is surprisingly high.

Antibiotic resistance is currently seen as a clinical problem for doctors and hospitals, rather than a more general health issue. The key to overcoming it is reframing resistance as a problem of public health importance and getting the public more engaged, as has been done with hand washing. Rather than patients asking for a prescription, we need them to ask "do I really need antibiotics for this?"

Superbugs are complex and pose a serious health threat. Only by working together, and prescribing smarter instead of broader, will we keep them at bay.

EVALUATING THE AUTHOR'S ARGUMENTS:

How does Trent Yarwood define the "tragedy of the commons?" Do you agree that the overuse of antibiotics by both physicians and patients exemplifies the tragedy of the commons? Explain.

Viewpoint

2

New Antibiotics Must Be Researched and Developed

Bob Corker and Richard Blumenthal

"We are in a real-life race against the super bugs, and we are losing."

The following viewpoint is by Republican US senator from Tennessee Bob Corker and Democratic US senator from Connecticut Richard Blumenthal. These legislators argue in favor of the Generating Antibiotic Incentives Now (GAIN) Act, legislation that would promote the development of new antibiotics. As the authors explain, pharmaceutical companies do not conduct much research on antibiotics because these medicines do not generate large profits. Since most people take antibiotics only for a short time, these drugs are not as profitable as are medicines used for chronic conditions. Corker and Blumenthal propose that Congress provide economic incentives and a quicker approval process to help spur the creation of badly needed new antibiotics.

I magine you are recovering from a routine surgery only to find yourself fighting for your life a few days later because of a bacterial infection that was acquired as a result of the procedure. To make matters worse, traditional medicines are proving ineffective at battling the infection.

This frightening scenario is an emerging reality as these "super bugs"—named so for their resistance to known antibiotics—are becoming more pervasive throughout the country and the world.

Reports from the Centers for Disease Control and Prevention indicate that MRSA, methicillin-resistant *Staphylococcus aureus*, is responsible for more than 17,000 deaths in the United States each year—more than AIDS—and that all 50 states have seen rates of antibiotic-resistant *E. coli* infections double in less than 10 years. A lesser-known bug, Acinetobacter, has infected more than 700 of our troops serving in Iraq since 2003, and the numbers continue to rise.

FAST FACT

When the costs of drug development increased in the 1990s, many pharmaceutical companies abandoned research on antibiotics, according to the American Council on Science and Health.

Jamel's Story

This disturbing trend is made all the more alarming by the devastating health consequences felt by patients. Jamel Sawyer, a former college football player from Norwalk, Conn., knows the crippling impact all too well after contracting an antibiotic-resistant Staph infection. After multiple

Decline in Food and Drug Administration (FDA) Approval of New Antibiotic Agents

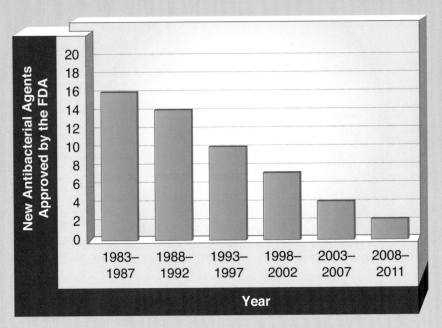

Taken from: Infectious Diseases Society of America.

rounds of antibiotic treatment, Jamel was left paralyzed from the waist down. Failing to fight back means bacteria like the kind that changed Jamel's life will continue to endanger patients across the country.

The history of antibiotics has repeated itself: Drugs are discovered but natural bacterial evolution increasingly renders them ineffective in treating infections. Overuse of antibiotics in humans or animals could be contributing to the ability of germs to mutate with increasing strength against our available medicines.

The Antibiotic Arms Race

Encouraging prescribers to use antibiotics only when patients really need them is important to extend the effectiveness of the antibiotics we have now, but this is not enough. Staying ahead in the arms race against super bugs is a constant challenge, especially when you consider that it takes researchers on average more than 10 years to develop just one new drug.

Research and development of new antibiotics present unique scientific and economic obstacles. The financial disincentives to create new antibiotics are significant, because they are only taken for a period of days or weeks, unlike cholesterol-reducing statins or other medicines used to treat lifelong conditions. New antibiotics are not "blockbuster" drugs, lacking the long-term revenue potential of more routinely administered products. Consequently, the number of new drugs in our antibiotic pipeline has run dry, and Food and Drug Administration [FDA] approval of new antibiotics has decreased by 70 percent since the mid-1980s.

To address this growing public health threat, we recently introduced the Generating Antibiotic Incentives Now (GAIN) Act, bipartisan legislation that seeks to spur development of new antibiotics. Without putting federal dollars at stake, the bill provides the necessary economic incentives so innovators and pharmaceutical companies are willing to make the necessary investments. These incentives include longer exclusive marketing rights and a quicker, streamlined FDA regulatory review process. Expanding these drugs' exclusive access to the market would compensate for lower return from sales, and prompt, expedited consideration by the FDA would benefit patients as well as drug-makers, many of them small business innovators across the country.

A Necessary Step

Other steps should be taken to fight the spread of super bugs—including more prudent use of antibiotics and more effective infection prevention measures in our hospitals and healthcare centers—but passage of the GAIN Act is a necessary step that can be taken now. The proposal has broad bipartisan support in both houses of Congress, which in itself is an unusual and encouraging fact.

The bill has also been endorsed by 49 organizations across the country, including St Jude's Children's Research Hospital in Memphis, Tenn. In a letter expressing support for the GAIN Act, Dr. William Evans, the director and CEO of St. Jude, wrote: "We don't want

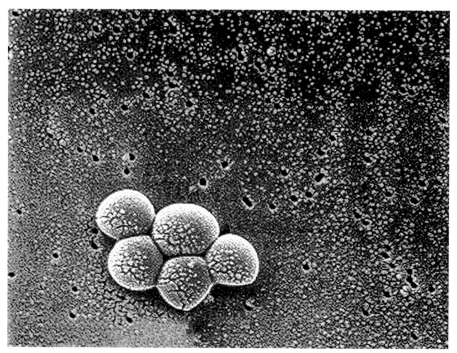

An electron micrograph depicts a group of methicillin-resistant Staphylococcus aureus *(MRSA) bacteria. MRSA is responsible for more than seventeen thousand deaths a year in the United States.*

to find ourselves in a situation in which we have been able to save a child's life after a cancer diagnosis, only to lose them to an untreatable multi-drug resistant infection."

We are in a real-life race against the super bugs, and we are losing. We must harness nature and American ingenuity to win.

EVALUATING THE AUTHOR'S ARGUMENTS:

Bob Corker and Richard Blumenthal contend that economic incentives would encourage pharmaceutical companies to research, develop, and create new antibiotics. Do you agree? Or do you think that promoting economic incentives for antibiotics could have negative consequences? Explain your answer.

Alternatives to Antibiotics Must Be Researched and Developed

Taylor McClean

"The government should provide more incentives to motivate scientists and especially pharmaceutical companies to invest in developing [alternatives to antibiotics]."

In the selection that follows Taylor McClean argues in favor of an alternative way to treat bacterial infections: bacteriophages, also known simply as "phages." Phages—viruses that kill bacteria—can be more effective than antibiotics at fighting bacterial infections, the author maintains; for example, while an antibiotic becomes less effective once bacteria develop resistance, a phage can respond to the bacteria's resistance and develop new ways to kill it. At present, very few companies are working on phages. McClean contends that the US government should provide economic incentives to scientists and pharmaceutical companies to speed up the development of this important new therapy. At the time of writing, McClean was a senior at Guilford College in Greensboro, North Carolina, majoring in biology.

AS YOU READ, CONSIDER THE FOLLOWING QUESTIONS:

1. For how long have scientists known about bacteriophages, according to the author?
2. What was the success rate for bacteriophage treatment at the Phage Therapy Center from 1987 to 1999, as stated by McClean?
3. What is one main problem with phage therapy, according to the author?

Over the years, we have become increasingly dependent on antibiotics to fight bacterial infections, but now more and more bacteria have developed resistance to these drugs. We need a new way to fight bacterial infections, and one way could be through bacteriophages. The use of bacteriophages as a new drug was first demonstrated in an experiment by Carl Merril and Richard Carlton, where mice were injected with *Escherichia coli* [*E. coli*] and then treated with bacteriophages that target the bacteria. The mice that did not receive any bacteriophage treatment died, while those that did had much higher survival rates. This is proof that bacteriophages could be and are becoming a legitimate form of anti-bacterial treatment (Travis, 2002).

Despite the promise of bacteriophages, little research has been done on them in the United States; the center of phage research and therapy is located in Eastern Europe. This paper therefore proposes that to encourage bacteriophage research in order to eventually lessen our dependence on antibiotics, we need to offer more monetary incentives in the form of governmental grants. Bacteriophages should also be fast tracked (a process that speeds up the review of a drug for serious medical conditions and that meets an unmet medical need) and submitted to priority review (drug proposal is reviewed within 6 months) (FDA, 2010).

How Bacteriophages Work

Bacteriophages (phages) are viruses that infect bacteria. They have a single type nucleic acid, a protein coat which surrounds the nucleic acid, a tail to inject the DNA or RNA into the host, and tail fibers to help attach to the host. Bacteriophages are specific—each one recognizes a different receptor that allows it to bind. They cannot bind and infect eukaryotic cells [cells that have a distinct, membrane-bound nucleus], therefore they only affect bacteria. (Tortura, 2010).

Bacteriophages used for phage therapy replicate using a lytic [degrading] cycle. In this form, the bacteriophage first attaches to a specific receptor site on a bacterial cell. It then injects its DNA or RNA into the host by releasing phage lysozyme [a molecule-breaking enzyme] through its tail, which degrades a portion of the cell wall. The tail sheath contracts, making the tail core drive through the cell wall and into the plasma membrane, where the nucleic acid is released. Biosynthesis of the viral nucleic acid then begins. The host DNA is degraded and protein synthesis is stopped as the phage DNA or RNA takes over the cell, using the host nucleotides and enzymes to replicate the phage's DNA/RNA. After this, the phage uses the machinery of the cell to make viral proteins, which happens exactly the same way as if the bacterial cell were making its own proteins, except viral RNA is now transcribed, not bacterial. The phage DNA/RNA and capsids [protein shell around the nucleus] assemble, lysozyme is synthesized within the cell to break down the cell wall again, and the new viruses are released. The bacteria cell is dead, while the newly made viruses can move on to infect other cells. (Tortura, 2010.)

Pros of Bacteriophages

A review of a study by [B.R.] Levin and [J.J.] Bull (1995) found that not only do bacteriophages work to fight bacterial infections, but that they can work better than antibiotics. Once administered, antibiotics degrade over time, while phages (if given before the bacteria reach a lethal level) have the ability to reproduce. This means that while antibiotics may become less effective over time, bacteriophages remain consistently effective and can therefore better clear bacteria. (Levin and Bull, 1995).

Phages also evolve along with the bacteria that they infect. This means that when the host evolves to protect itself against the virus, the virus responds by evolving so that it can still attack the host. Antibiotics cannot do this—if bacteria is resistant to it, there is no way for the antibiotic to change unless we modify it in the lab, which can take many months or years.

Current Use of Bacteriophages

Scientists have known about bacteriophages and their potential to fight bacteria since the early 1900's. With the discovery of antibiotics, however, the focus changed and the only ongoing research is in Eastern Europe, in former Soviet Union territories (Levin and Bull, 1995). Today, the main center of phage therapy and research is the Phage Therapy Center in the Republic of Georgia. The Phage Therapy Center treats patients with bacterial infections that are unresponsive to antibiotics and specializes in acute and chronic infections like laryngitis and acne, infections where circulation is poor (in diabetes patients, for example), and infections with bacteria that are highly resistant such as methicillin resistant *Staphylococcus aureus* (MRSA) (phagetherapy center.com). In order to treat patients, scientists at the Phage Therapy Center first collect a bacterial sample to determine the strain of bacteria and to characterize it. They then develop a phage mixture that is specific to the bacterial infection and work with other doctors and surgeons to successfully treat the disease. This treatment works well against these bacterial infections, especially those that are highly resistant to antibiotics. For example, from the years 1987 to 1999, the center treated 1307 people and had an 85% success rate and 10% improvement rate (the rest had no effect). Success rates for specific diseases ranged from 61% (varicose ulcers of lower extremities) to 100% (purulent meningitis), with most diseases having success rates in the 80 and 90 percents (phagetherapycenter.com).

FAST FACT

Polish studies have found phages (viruses that kill bacteria) to be effective in treating meningitis in newborns and skin infections caused by staph and *E. coli* bacteria.

While there is nothing like the Phage Therapy Center in Georgia located in the United States, there are American companies that are working with bacteriophages. Intralytic, Inc. is probably one of the closest to developing a product, as it has recently obtained a grant from the US Army to develop a probiotic derived from phages to fight against *Shigella,* called ShigActive. They also have two products in development that target *Staphylococcus aureus* and *Acineobacter bau-*

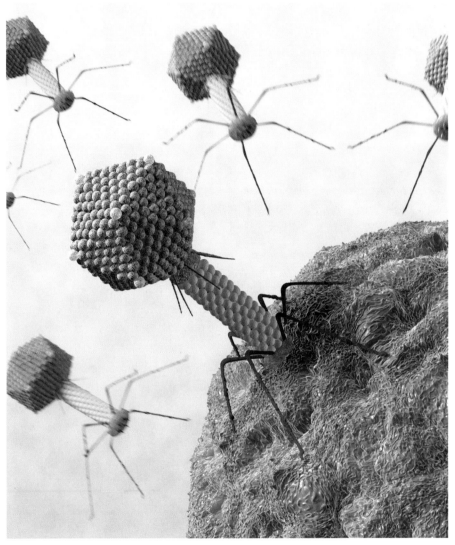

Bacteriophages attack a bacterium. Called "phages" for short, they are viruses that infect bacteria. Scientists use these phages to help control drug-resistant bacteria.

mannii, along with several other products to help prevent contamination in food processing plants and to reduce bacteria in animals, such as chicken and cattle (intralytix.com). Another company, Epitopix, has developed similar products to reduce bacteria in cattle, specifically *E. coli,* and has obtained a license from the United States to market its phage-derived product. Products such as these intend to reduce the risk of food poisoning in humans by diminishing the amount of bacteria in the animals themselves (Byrne, 2009). While these companies

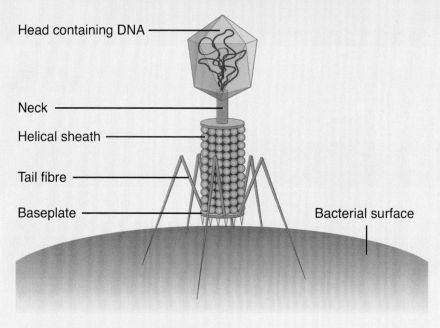

Diagram of Bacteriophage

Head containing DNA

Neck

Helical sheath

Tail fibre

Baseplate

Bacterial surface

Taken from: Thomas Hausler. "Viruses vs. Superbugs: A Solution to the Antibiotics Crisis?" 2007.
www.bacteriophagetherapy.info.

have made developments with bacteriophages, these developments are still little in comparison to the success of the Phage Therapy Center in Georgia on treating human infections.

Cons of Bacteriophages

The Phage Therapy Center in Georgia reports that there are fewer side effects with their treatment than with antibiotics, since phages are more specific and do not disrupt the natural bacteria in the body. As with antibiotics though, there is still the possibility that phages could kill too many bacteria too fast, causing the bacteria to release dangerous levels of endotoxins which then make the patient sick. One of the main problems with phage therapy, however, is the cost. While it is easier to develop a new phage than it is a new antibiotic, treatment at the Phage Therapy Center in Georgia ranges from $2,500 US dollars for outpatient care to $20,000 for in-patient treatment, in addition to travel costs. In addition, if the bacteria that the patient has is resistant to the phages the center has, there is an extra charge to develop a specific, unique phage for that person. This brings up another problem with bacteriophages—bacteria can become resistant to them just like antibiotics. The difference, however, is that even if a bacteria is resistant to one phage, the phage can respond to the bacteria's resistance and evolve to infect it again in a new way (phagetherapycenter.com).

Another problem with bacteriophages is the way they are administered, at least in places like the Phage Therapy Center. Patients are given a "cocktail" of phages that may vary between regions and hospitals, and the FDA [Food and Drug Administration] is not set up to handle such a system but to monitor one specific drug that is not constantly changing (Kantor, 2006). In addition, many pharmaceutical companies are not interested in developing new drugs that will treat a onetime infection—they are more interested in treatments that are needed long-term for chronic diseases like diabetes, as this means more profit for them (Totura, 2010). . . .

Policy Proposal

Using bacteriophages to fight bacterial infections means that any such product will be treated as a new drug, therefore falling under the FDA's jurisdiction. So far, the FDA seems to have reasonable guidelines for developing new drugs, but the only problem is the length of time it takes to get approval, especially since this is a way to treat serious diseases for which there is no current effective therapy. Therfore, bacteriophage therapy should be fast-tracked and submitted to priority review. In addition, the government should provide more incentives to motivate scientists and especially pharmaceutical companies to invest in developing these products.

References

Barnum, S., *Biotechnology: An Introduction.* Miami University, 2005.

Tortora, G., Funke, B., Cae, C., *Microbiology: An Introduction.* San Francisco: Pearson Education Inc., 2010.

Kantor, A., "U.S. Needs to Open Eyes to Phage Therapy," *USA Today* (2006). http://www.usatoday.com/tech/columnist/andrew kantor/2006-07-06-phageo-therapy_x.htm.

Byrne, J., "Vaccine Targeted at E. coli Gets First U.S. License," Meatpress.com (2009). http://www.meatprocess.com/Safety-Legislation/Vaccine-targeted-at-E.coli-gets-first-US-licence.

Levin, B., Bull, J., "Phage Therapy Revisited: The Population Biology of a Bacterial Infection and Its Treatment with Bacteriophage Antibiotics," *The American Naturalist.*

Castelvecchi, D., "Biowarfare: Engineered Virus Can Invade Bacterial Film," *Science News.*

The Phage Therapy Center Home Page. October 27, 2010. http://www.phagetherapycenter.com/pii/PatientServlet?command=static_home.

The Intralytix, Inc. Home Page, October 27, 2010. http://www.intralytix.com/index.htm.

The Epitopix Home Page, October 27, 2010. http://www.epitopix.com/.

Regulatory Information: US FDA, October 27, 2010. http://www.fda.gov/RegulatoryInformation/Legislation/FederalFoodDrugandCosmeticActFDCAct/FDCActChapterVDrugsandDevices/ucm108125.htm.

EVALUATING THE AUTHOR'S ARGUMENTS:

In this viewpoint, Taylor McClean discusses the advantages as well as the disadvantages of bacteriophages as an alternative to antibiotics. Identify and list the pros and cons of bacteriophages. Given what you have read elsewhere in this text, do the advantages of phages outweigh their disadvantages? Why or why not?

The Overuse of Antibiotics on Factory Farms Must Be Discouraged

"Antimicrobial drugs must be used 'judiciously' in both animal and human medicine to slow the development of resistance."

US Food and Drug Administration

In the following viewpoint the US Food and Drug Administration (FDA), using a question-and-answer format, outlines its plan for promoting careful and proper use of antibiotics in food-producing animals. Recognizing that the overuse of antibiotics creates drug-resistant bacteria, the FDA recommends that farmers use these drugs only to treat or prevent disease in animals. The FDA discourages the use of antibiotics to boost growth in animals and suggests that farmers consult veterinarians to ensure the judicious use of these important drugs. Part of the US Department of Health and Human Services, the FDA's goal is to protect public health by monitoring the safety of foods and medicines.

"FDA's Strategy on Antimicrobial Resistance: Questions and Answers," April 11, 2012, Food and Drug Administration.

AS YOU READ, CONSIDER THE FOLLOWING QUESTIONS:
1. How does the FDA define *antimicrobial drugs* in the viewpoint?
2. In what ways have antimicrobial drugs traditionally been used in food-producing animals, according to the author?
3. In the FDA's view, how can veterinarians help ensure careful use of antibiotics on farms?

T he Food and Drug Administration (FDA) is implementing a voluntary strategy to promote the judicious use in food-producing animals of antibiotics that are important in treating humans. The goal of the strategy is to protect public health and help curb the development of antimicrobial resistance and in turn help to reduce the number of infections in humans that are difficult to treat because existing antibiotics have become ineffective.

What are antimicrobial drugs and antimicrobial resistance?

"Antimicrobial drugs" include all drugs that work against a variety of microorganisms, such as bacteria, viruses, fungi, and parasites. "Antimicrobial resistance" is when bacteria or other microbes become resistant to the effects of a drug after being exposed to them. This means that the drug, and similar drugs, will no longer work against those bacteria. If resistant bacteria enter the food supply, drugs normally used to treat people infected with those bacteria may not work.

FAST FACT

The FDA reports that 30.6 million pounds of antibiotics were administered to livestock in the United States in 2010.

Judicious Use of Antibiotics
Why is FDA taking this action?

It is well established scientifically that all uses of antimicrobial drugs, in both humans and animals, contribute to the development of antimicrobial resistance, and that this is an important public health concern. Experts agree that antimicrobial drugs must be used "judiciously" in both animal and human medicine to slow the development of resistance.

What is "judicious use" and what are FDA's recommendations?
"Judicious use" is using an antimicrobial drug appropriately and only when necessary; Based on a thorough review of the available scientific information, FDA recommends that use of medically important antimicrobial drugs in food-producing animals be limited to situations where the use of these drugs is necessary for ensuring animal health, and their use includes veterinary oversight or consultation. FDA believes that using medically important antimicrobial drugs to increase production in food-producing animals is not a judicious use.

Why did FDA decide to do this now?
FDA has worked with many stakeholder groups and the U.S. Department of Agriculture (USDA) to develop a strategy that will

Vets treat a calf with antimicrobial resistance. Such resistance is caused by overuse of antibiotics in animals, many contend.

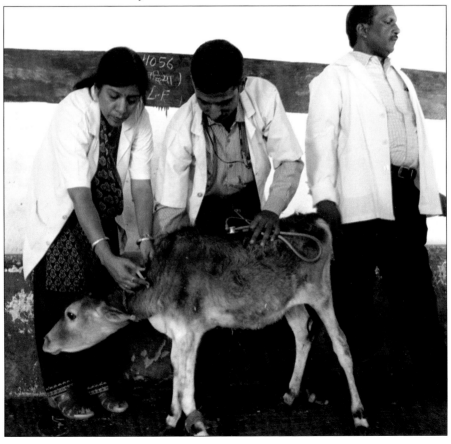

be successful in reducing antimicrobial resistance while minimizing adverse impacts on animal health and disruption to the animal agricultural industry. In June 2010, FDA released a draft guidance document explaining its recommendations for change and in the interim period sought and received input from various stakeholders, including the animal pharmaceutical industry, animal feed industry, veterinary and animal producer communities, consumer advocacy groups and USDA. . . .

Focusing on Important Medicines

Which antimicrobial drugs used in food-producing animals are the focus of FDA's strategy?

The voluntary strategy is primarily focused on medically important antimicrobial drugs that:

- Were approved prior to the issuance of Guidance 152, *Evaluating the Safety of Antimicrobial New Animal Drugs with Regard to Their Microbiological Effects on Bacteria of Human Health Concern*, published in October 2003.
- Are used in food-producing animals to increase feed efficiency and promote growth;
- Are available over-the-counter (OTC), and therefore, can be given without a veterinarian's involvement; and
- Are given continuously through the feed or water to entire herds or flocks of animals. . . .

How have antimicrobial drugs traditionally been used in food-producing animals?

Antimicrobial drugs that are FDA-approved for use in food-producing animals are normally used to:

- Treat or control an on-going infectious disease;
- Prevent an infectious disease before an outbreak occurs; or
- Increase production by making the animal gain weight faster and by improving the animal's ability to convert the food it eats (improved feed efficiency). With these agricultural production uses, typically no disease is present and no outbreak is anticipated to occur. These drugs are given to animals to enhance the production of animal-derived food products.

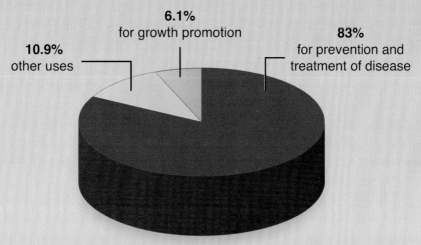

Antibiotic Usage in Food-Producing Animals

6.1%
for growth promotion

10.9%
other uses

83%
for prevention and
treatment of disease

Taken from: Jeff Fowle; "Food Inc. Correction #1—Antibiotics." Common Sense Agriculture's Blog, June 22, 2009. commonsenseagriculture.com/tag/antibiotics.

Veterinary Oversight

Why is the involvement of a veterinarian important?

Most of the antimicrobial drugs approved for use in food-producing animals in feed or water are over-the-counter products. Including veterinary oversight or consultation when these drugs are used in food-producing animals is an important way to ensure judicious use. This is because judicious use involves accurately identifying bacterial disease that is present or likely to be present and selecting the suitable antimicrobial drug. In the case of prevention, judicious use includes a consideration of relevant factors for determining the risk of a specific bacterial disease. FDA understands that veterinary oversight or consultation varies due to many factors, such as geographic location of the farm and different animal production methods. Sometimes, veterinarians directly diagnose and treat animals, while other times, they periodically visit and consult with an animal producer to customize a disease management protocol for that producer's herd or flock.

How will greater veterinary oversight help ensure that the use of medically important antimicrobial drugs for disease prevention purposes is appropriate and judicious? Can you give an example?

We believe that veterinary expertise can determine whether the use of antimicrobials for preventive purposes is appropriate in a particular situation and, thus, would be considered judicious. We also believe that veterinarians are uniquely qualified to determine which specific diseases or conditions are likely to be present and to determine which specific approved drug or combination drug is most appropriate, based on factors such as the mode of antibacterial action, drug distribution in specific tissues, and the duration of effective drug levels at the site of infection. From FDA's standpoint, the administration of antimicrobial drugs to animals when a veterinarian determines that there is a risk of a specific disease based on the presence of risk factors such as the stress of transport, environmental factors, or weaning, would be considered judicious use for prevention. For example, if a veterinarian determines, based on the client's production practices and history, that a group of weaned beef calves arriving at a feedlot in bad weather after a lengthy transport is likely to develop an infection, preventively treating this group with an antimicrobial approved for prevention of that bacterial infection would be considered a judicious use. On the other hand, FDA would not consider administration of a drug to apparently healthy animals in the absence of any information that such animals were at risk of a specific disease to be a judicious use for prevention.

EVALUATING THE AUTHOR'S ARGUMENTS:

In this viewpoint the US Food and Drug Administration recommends stopping the use of antibiotics to boost growth in food-producing animals like poultry and cattle. Do you think that this recommendation will be effective in reducing drug-resistant infections? Why or why not? Cite from the text in defending your answer.

Viewpoint
5

The Overuse of Antibiotics on Factory Farms Must Be Banned

"Ban preventive use of antibiotics to require the industry to raise animals in a manner that assures both public and animal health."

Robert S. Lawrence

In April 2011 the US Food and Drug Administration (FDA) asked the farming industry to voluntarily stop using antibiotics to make animals grow faster. This use of antibiotics, the FDA claimed, fosters the development of drug-resistant bacteria. In the following viewpoint Robert S. Lawrence contends that this FDA action has not stopped the overuse of antibiotics in food animal production. Farmers are still feeding animals antibiotics to prevent diseases that are caused by unclean and overcrowded conditions. In the author's opinion, these preventative antibiotics should be banned—and this would force farmers to raise animals in healthier ways. Healthier conditions for farm animals would do away with the need for excess antibiotics and, in turn, would curb the spread of drug-resistant infections. Lawrence is director of the Johns Hopkins Center for a Livable Future in Baltimore, Maryland.

Robert S. Lawrence, "The FDA Did Not Do Enough to Restrict Antibiotic Use in Animals," *The Atlantic*, April 16, 2012. Copyright © 2012 by The Atlantic. All rights reserved. Reproduced by permission.

What Should Be Done to Stop the Spread of Drug-Resistant Bacteria?   97

1. How did animal agriculture change in the second half of the twentieth century, according to Lawrence?
2. What factors are lacking in current animal production practices, in the author's opinion?
3. As reported by Lawrence, what happened in Denmark after the country banned the misuse of antibiotics in its swine industry?

"FDA takes steps to protect public health," blared the Food and Drug Administration (FDA) press release announcing the release of voluntary guidance documents on Wednesday [April 11, 2012]. The documents outline how antibiotics should—and should not—be used in food animal production to slow the development of antibiotic-resistant bacteria. The agency has trumpeted the documents as the beginning of the end of the misuse of these drugs on farms.

The FDA missed the point, however. While the documents call for ending the use of antibiotics to make animals grow faster, they endorse the continued use of these drugs to compensate for overcrowded and unsanitary conditions and prevent disease at the industrial operations that produce most food animals in this country. The preventive or "prophylactic" use of antibiotics is similar to their use for growth promotion, involving comparable low doses that are equally culpable in the development of antibiotic resistance.

The FDA calls preventive use "necessary to assure animal health." Left unaddressed is what makes this use "necessary." The industrial model of food animal production increases animals' exposure to bacterial pathogens and weakens the animals' immune system through overcrowding and the suppression of normal animal behaviors, leaving them susceptible to infections without the continuous administration of low doses of antibiotics. Rather than ban preventive use of antibiotics to require the industry to raise animals in a manner that assures both public and animal health, the guidance document accommodates an industry that undermines both.

The Low-Hanging Fruit

The guidance documents spell out two principles for the "judicious use" of antibiotics in food animal production. First, antibiotics should only be used when "necessary to assure animal health." This means the treatment, control, and prevention of disease, but not growth promotion, according to the FDA. Second, antibiotics should be available only when prescribed by a veterinarian and not sold over the counter.

The FDA had previously approved the use of several antibiotics for growth promotion. Rather than forcibly withdraw these approvals—a move that many drug companies would oppose—the agency believes it can persuade drug companies to voluntarily change existing approvals to comply with the guidance documents. The Animal Health Institute, an industry lobby group, has said it supports the guidances, as have several pharmaceutical executives.

We can expect the FDA and drug companies to revoke existing approvals for growth promotion over the next several years. Likewise, the agency and the drug industry will gradually end the sale of antibiotics over the counter.

Will the Food Industry Comply?

The effect of these actions on the use of antibiotics will depend in part on whether or not the food animal industry complies with the changes. There is good reason to doubt the food animal industry will comply. A recent study by the Johns Hopkins Center for a Livable Future, which I direct, strongly suggests that the poultry industry has continued to use a class of antibiotics known as fluoroquinolones, despite an FDA ban on the use of these drugs in chickens and turkeys. These findings raise an important question: how can we expect the industry to comply with voluntary guidance documents if it does not follow existing law?

FAST FACT

Following Denmark's lead, the European Union limited the use of antibiotics on farms in 2006.

Even if the food animal industry complies, however, the misuse of antibiotics will continue, because the guidance documents endorse the use of these drugs for disease prevention. Like growth promotion, this means feeding small quantities of antibiotics to food animals throughout their lives—a practice that has been shown time and again to select

Bacteria Are Resistant to Many Common Antibiotics

Bacteria	Description
Acinetobacter	Found in soil and water, often causes infections in seriously ill hospital patients.
Anthrax	Spread by infected animals or potentially bioterrorist weapons.
Campylobacter	A pathogen common to chicken products.
Gonorrhea	A sexually transmitted disease.
Group B strep	Common bacteria in newborns, the elderly, and adults with other illnesses.
Klebsiella pneumonia	Bacteria that can lead to pneumonia, wound and surgical site infections, and meningitis.
Methicillin-resistant *Staphyloccus aureus* (MRSA)	A superbug that can progress from a superficial skin infection to a life-threatening infection in bones, joints, blood stream, heart valves, lungs, or wounds.
Neisseria meningitides	A leading cause of bacterial meningitis in children and young adults.
Shigella	An infectious disease caused by *Shigella* bacteria.
Streptococcus pneumoniae	A leading cause of sinusitis, pneumonia, ear infections, bacteremia.
Tuberculosis (TB)	Both "multidrug resistant" and "extensively drug-resistant" forms of TB are now being seen.
Typhoid fever	A life-threatening illness caused by the *Salmonella typhi* bacteria.
Vancomycin-resistant enterococci (VRE)	Infection that occurs in hospitals and is resistant to an "antibiotic of last resort."
Vancomycin-resistant *Staphylococcus aureus* (VRSA)	Various strains of staph bacteria that are resistant to vancomycin.

Taken from: Joseph Mercola. "What State Uses More Antibiotics on Livestock than Entire U.S. on Humans?" mercola.com, July 9, 2011. http://articles.mercola.com/sites/articles/archive/2011/07/09/what-uses-more-antibiotics-on-livestock-than-entire-us-on-humans.aspx.

for antibiotic resistance. It is quite different from the preventive use of antibiotics in human medicine, which is relatively rare and involves the use of full doses for short durations.

Although growth promotion may be phased out, the drug and food animal industries will not give up the use of antibiotics for disease prevention so easily, as preventive use of these drugs is essential to the industrial model of food animal production.

The Industrial Model

The second half of the twentieth century witnessed the transformation of animal agriculture. Beginning in the 1940s, small independent farms were subsumed by industrial operations controlled by a small handful of large corporations. Since the 1950s, the number of food animals produced in the United States has doubled, while the number of production sites has declined by 80 percent. This efficiency is unprecedented, but the methods used to achieve it have left animals exceedingly vulnerable to bacterial infection and disease.

The industrial operations that dominate modern food animal production confine hundreds and often thousands of animals in overcrowded and unsanitary facilities. In a single poultry house, tens of thousands of chickens or turkeys may be packed beak-to-beak. The enormous quantity of waste these animals generate is not removed until the birds reach market weight and a new flock arrives (about once every 45 days). Left for weeks, feces pile up in poultry bedding, constantly exposing chickens and turkeys to pathogens and harmful chemicals.

Raised indoors, poultry and swine cannot access the traditional forage for which their digestive systems have evolved. The animals instead receive artificial feeds based on corn and soybeans. The stress of overcrowding, poor nutrition, and the denial of normal animal behaviors weaken the immune systems of the animals, leaving them more susceptible to infection by the pathogens in their waste and on the animals with which they are cloistered.

The economic success of a production system so detrimental to its product is counterintuitive. The secret to its success has been, in no small part, the continuous feeding of small doses of antibiotics to food animals throughout their lives. These drugs help animals grow faster, and they also stave off infections linked to the squalid conditions in which food animals are raised. The misuse of antibiotics by the food animal industry is not just a means to make a quick buck; misusing these drugs is the lynchpin of the industrial model.

Missing the Point

If antibiotics could no longer be used for disease prevention, the food animal production industry would be forced to reform its production practices to raise healthy animals in other ways. The preventive use of antibiotics would no longer be "necessary." By eliding [omitting] this fact in its guidance documents, the FDA has built public health policy around the needs of the industry rather than require the industry to reform itself to assure both human and animal health.

The guidance document defines disease prevention as follows: "the administration of antimicrobial drugs to animals, none of which are [sic] exhibiting clinical signs of disease, *in a situation where disease is likely to occur if the drug is not administered*" (emphasis added). The question of someone concerned about animal health should be, Why is disease likely to occur in the absence of an antibiotic? Asked the same question in the context of human health, an epidemiologist might consider such factors as sanitation, housing, and nutrition—three aspects of industrial food animal production that are sadly lacking.

The agency gives a revealing example of disease prevention: "if a veterinarian determines, *based on a client's production practices* and herd health history, that cattle being transported *or otherwise stressed* are more likely to develop a certain bacterial infection" (emphasis added), preventive use of an antibiotic may be recommended.

This example dances around important questions too. How might "production practices" contribute to the risk of developing bacterial infections? How might animals be "otherwise stressed" in ways that increase their susceptibility to infection and disease? These questions suggest a third: why should the food animal industry be allowed to use antibiotics to compensate for poor production practices and the stresses animals incur as a result?

In an earlier draft of the guidance document, the FDA described how a veterinarian should determine the appropriateness of using antibiotics for disease prevention. An important criterion was the

These turkeys are being raised without the use of antibiotics on a US farm in an attempt to help reduce the production of drug-resistant bacteria.

availability of "evidence that no reasonable alternatives for intervention exist." The implication is clear. If there is evidence that improving the living conditions and nutrition of food animals could reduce the occurrence of bacterial infections, it would be better to do so than to use antibiotics in ways that endanger the public health.

Alternatives Work

Denmark provides clear evidence of alternatives. In 2000, the country banned the misuse of antibiotics over the strenuous objections of the Danish swine industry. There was an initial uptick in animal morbidity and mortality until the industry gave the animals more space, delayed weaning, fed them more nutritious diets, and made other improvements. Denmark remains the top exporter of pork products in the world today. FDA never seriously considered such alternatives, however. The agency tellingly removed the criterion from the final version of the guidance document.

The use of antibiotics to make food animals grow faster appears to be on its last legs, although much will depend on how quickly drug companies comply with the guidance documents and whether the food animal industry complies at all. For public health advocates, the fight now moves to the use of these drugs for disease prevention. This is a much steeper hill to climb: their misuse lies at the heart of industrial food animal production, and the FDA has abdicated its responsibility to stop it. The agency would like to declare victory and move on. It is clear that the agency, and we, have work to do.

EVALUATING THE AUTHOR'S ARGUMENTS:

Robert S. Lawrence maintains that the Food and Drug Administration (FDA) has not done enough to restrict the use of antibiotics in food-animal production. Where do the FDA recommendations to the agricultural industry fall short, in his opinion? What does he suggest as an alternative? Compare Lawrence's recommendations to the ones offered in the previous viewpoint by the FDA. Which viewpoint offers the sounder advice, in your opinion?

Antibacterial Soaps Should Be Banned

Statesman.com

"Antibacterial soap . . . contributes to drug resistance in bacteria."

There is no evidence that antibacterial soaps prevent the spread of disease better than regular soap, argues the author in the following viewpoint. Furthermore, triclosan, the antibacterial ingredient in many antibacterial soaps, promotes the development of antibiotic-resistant bacteria. Since triclosan-containing antibacterial soaps can end up doing more harm than good, they should be banned, the author concludes. Statesman.com is the website of the *Austin American-Statesman*, a Texas daily newspaper.

AS YOU READ, CONSIDER THE FOLLOWING QUESTIONS:

1. As stated by Statesman.com, what percentage of Americans over the age of five have triclosan in their urine?
2. Where is triclosan useful, in the author's opinion?
3. How many Americans die each year from antibiotic-resistant strains of *Clostridium difficile*, according to Statesman.com?

The resolution passed Tuesday [March 6, 2012,] by the University of Texas' (UT) student government calling for administrators to ban antibacterial soap from campus might sound silly, but there is merit to the effort.

Like many consumer products, antibacterial soap is more a fact of marketing than of need or science. There is no evidence that antibacterial soap checks the spread of germs on campus, at work or at home any better than regular soap. There is evidence, however, suggesting that antibacterial soap—specifically triclosan, the antibacterial agent in antibacterial soap—disrupts hormone levels in animals and contributes to drug resistance in bacteria.

FAST FACT

There is no data proving that antibacterial products prevent the spread of infection better than products with no antibacterial additives, according to the National Institutes of Health.

A Coming Trend

While the vote by UT's student government is easy to mock—more busybodies goofily targeting the seemingly trivial—the resolution could be ahead of a coming trend. As more studies and attention focus on triclosan, it's easy to see the chemical going the way of bisphenol A, the chemical in plastic bottles that was the subject of public scrutiny a few years ago and which has largely disappeared from many products.

UT, prompted by concerns about antibacterial soap's cost compared with regular soap and its potential environmental effects, stopped using antibacterial soap in most restrooms in 2008, as the *American-Statesman*'s Farzad Mashhood reported. . . . In a way, a ban would complete a process already begun.

The Food and Drug Administration currently does not consider triclosan harmful to humans, but the agency isn't sure how safe the chemical is, either, and has been closely reviewing it for the past two years. The results of the FDA's review are expected to be released in the next few months. [On December 16, 2013, the FDA issued a proposed rule requiring manufacturers to substantiate claims of effectiveness and long-term safety of antibacterial soaps.]

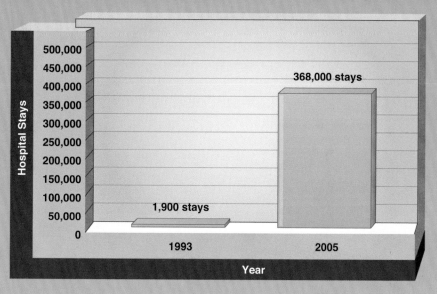

Hospital Stays for MRSA (Methicillin-Resistant *Staphylococcus Aureus*) in the United States

368,000 stays

1,900 stays

Hospital Stays

500,000
450,000
400,000
350,000
300,000
250,000
200,000
150,000
100,000
50,000
0

1993   2005

Year

Taken from: Michelle Castillo. "Less than Half of Americans Recognize Antibiotic Overuse as a Problem." *CBS News,* November 13, 2012.

Examining Triclosan

The Centers for Disease Control and Prevention [CDC] published a study in 2009 which found that 75 percent of Americans older than 5 have triclosan in their urine. A University of Michigan study published in 2010 suggested that triclosan may contribute to allergies in young people.

Triclosan is used in thousands of products. Other than finding evidence that triclosan in toothpaste helps prevent gingivitis, the FDA has no evidence it provides any benefit in any other product.

The Centers for Disease Control and Prevention also has been looking at triclosan. According to the CDC, "Antibacterial-containing products have not been proven to prevent the spread of infection better than products that do not contain antibacterial chemicals."

There's a possible environmental effect, too. When you wash with soap that contains triclosan, the chemical goes down the drain to wastewater treatment plants. What isn't removed by the treatment

According to the Centers for Disease Control and Prevention, "Antibacterial-containing products have not been proven to prevent the spread of infection better than products that do not contain antibacterial chemicals."

plant winds up in rivers, creeks and other surface water, where it might interfere with the development of some wildlife.

Triclosan is useful in hospitals and other health care settings—it was invented in the early 1970s and used, for example, as a surgical scrub. But like antibiotics, which have been overprescribed for decades, the overuse of triclosan in consumer products might be contributing to antibiotic resistance.

A Public Health Issue

Resistance to antibiotics is an urgent public health issue, and drug companies are not keeping pace with the problem by developing new antibiotics to replace those that no longer work as well as they once did. The price of drug-resistant germs is more serious infections, longer stays in hospitals and the use of stronger antibiotics that can cause more serious side effects—all of which increase costs.

Here's how the CDC puts it: "People infected with drug-resistant organisms are more likely to have longer and more expensive hospital stays, and may be more likely to die as a result of the infection. When the drug of choice for treating their infection doesn't work, they require treatment with second- or third-choice drugs that may be less effective, more toxic and more expensive."

Coincidentally, the same day as the UT vote, the CDC released a report expressing alarm about the rise of antibiotic-resistant strains of *Clostridium difficile,* a bacteria that causes severe diarrhea. The bacteria infects hundreds of thousands of Americans each year, killing about 14,000.

Antibacterial soap's role in the development of antibiotic-resistant bacteria perhaps isn't as significant as the overuse of antibiotics in people and food animals, if it exists at all. But why take the risk when there appears to be little or no benefit?

Laugh at the student vote if you will, but if UT administrators agree to ban antibacterial soap from campus, they will have rid the university of a product that at best is unnecessary and at worst might cause more harm than good.

EVALUATING THE AUTHOR'S ARGUMENTS:

After reading this viewpoint by the Statesman.com, are you more likely or less likely to support a ban on antibacterial hand soap in your school or community? Explain.

Antibacterial Soaps Should Not Be Banned

Derek Hunter

"The antimicrobial agent [in antibacterial hand soaps] does not harm humans."

There is no proof that triclosan, the antimicrobial agent in some antibacterial hand soaps, harms people, writes Derek Hunter in the following viewpoint. Antibacterial soaps limit the spread of bacteria—especially during cold and flu season—which is why they are so popular. These soaps are also effective at preventing the spread of disease between patients and doctors in hospitals, the author points out. Liberal politicians calling for a ban on these soaps claim that they harm the environment, but they have no data to support their case, Hunter argues. Hunter is a columnist, radio host, and consultant based in Washington, D.C.

AS YOU READ, CONSIDER THE FOLLOWING QUESTIONS:

1. What percentage of American consumers use antimicrobial soap, according to the author?
2. According to Hunter, what event spurred the banning of the pesticide DDT?
3. Which groups really benefit from the use of antibacterial soaps, according to the author?

To say the government regulates everything is an understatement. Aside from the black market, which is only unregulated insofar as it avoids taxes and bypasses age restrictions on such things as alcohol (not including illegal products), there really isn't much in which the government doesn't have a hand. And now they're thinking about coming after your hand . . . well, your hand soap, anyway.

Antimicrobial hand soaps and body washes are very popular, especially in cold and flu season. They've been found to be effective in limiting the spread of bacteria, which is why they're so popular. But, like anything people like, there are people who don't like it, and the people who don't like something are rarely content until their will is imposed upon everyone else.

A recent survey found that 74 percent of consumers use antimicrobial hand soap, 84 percent have no concerns about it, and 67 percent would be upset if the government banned it.

In this case, the people who don't like it are the left-wing environmentalists who don't seem to like much of anything humans concoct to improve people's quality of life. Their usual modus operandi is being followed in this case. Rather than trying to make a case for or against something, these groups have taken to the courts. Why the courts? Because the government can't ban something, in this case the antimicrobial agent Triclosan, without proof of some sort that it's harmful, whereas the courts, let's just say they're a little less constrained.

No Proof of Harm

This hasn't stopped some liberal politicians from calling for a ban of Triclosan, too. Not wanting to be left behind in any potential hysteria, Congressman Ed Markey, the leading voice in Congress calling for regulating the Internet, and Congresswoman Louise Slaughter have called for a ban. Note Slaughter's letter and the artful use of phrases like "have raised concerns about possible environmental effects" and "potential effects on human health." That's a lot of qualifiers, but they're needed because there isn't any proof. But Congress so rarely lets proof get in the way of a good story.

FAST FACT

Several studies indicate that products containing triclosan kill up to 99.6 percent of germs.

The Natural Resources Defense Council (NRDC) is suing the Food and Drug Administration (FDA) in an attempt to get the FDA to move against Triclosan, even though the FDA's own testing has shown that the antimicrobial agent does not harm humans.

The public isn't buying it either. A recent survey found 74% of consumers use antimicrobial hand soap, 84% have no concerns about it and two-thirds would be upset if the government banned it. But, as illustrated by the health care debate and outcome last year [2010], what the public wants matters little to far too many people elected to represent their will.

The DDT Comparison

Why would a liberal environmental group be suing over something that helps prevent illness? Is it that they're simply anti-people? Well,

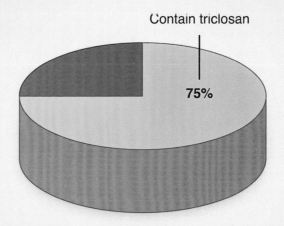

Percent of Liquid Soap Products Containing Triclosan

Contain triclosan

75%

Taken from: wiseGEEK. "What Is Triclosan?" 2013. www.wisegeek.com.

they claim it's harmful to humans and the environment, pretty much what they claim for everything they oppose, despite a lack of evidence. We've seen this before, with disastrous effects.

The pesticide DDT was used for years to control the mosquito population, the main source of the deadly disease malaria. DDT use effectively eliminated malaria from the United States and saved millions of lives around the world. Then a book came along and everything changed.

In 1962, biologist Rachel Carson published *Silent Spring*, in which she claimed that DDT and other pesticides caused cancer. From that book the modern environmental movement was born, and a race was on to ban DDT. In 1972, despite a lack of evidence that DDT causes cancer (something that hasn't been proven to this day), DDT was banned in the United States. The Stockholm Convention, which took effect in 2004, banned most uses of DDT worldwide. The ban strips us of our strongest weapon in the fight against malaria, a disease that takes nearly one million lives each year.

So, thanks to a ban sparked by an unproven theory, fanned by an environmental-industrial complex looking to make a name for itself and enforced by governments around the world, the best defense against malaria that is routinely used today is a net under which people sleep. That's right, a net over their beds. So people in tropical regions of the planet are protected from disease carrying mosquitoes . . . when they sleep.

It's little wonder that the number of malaria deaths continues to rise, DDT continues to be banned and environmentalists continue to not be very concerned.

Perspective Is Needed

Not that banning antimicrobial hand soap is the same as banning DDT, but that can be a matter of perspective.

In hospitals, antimicrobial hand soap has been shown to be effective in preventing the spread of diseases from patients to doctors, then to other patients. This is particularly important to the elderly, whose immune systems are susceptible to infection. Yet environmental groups, who claim bed nets are as effective as killing mosquitoes with DDT, claim regular soap is as effective as antimicrobial soap. This claim can be dismissed by logic alone. Let us hope we never find ourselves in a position to have hard data proving it.

EVALUATING THE AUTHOR'S ARGUMENTS:

Derek Hunter contends that environmental groups are wrongly calling for a ban on triclosan, an antibacterial ingredient in many hand soaps. Examine how he describes the motivations and arguments of those he disagrees with. Are these descriptions accurate or inaccurate, in your opinion? Why?

Facts About Antibiotics

Editor's note: These facts can be used in reports to add credibility when making important points or claims.

- Most antibiotics are derived from living organisms such as bacteria, fungi, and molds. Others are produced synthetically.
- There are 160 varieties of antibiotics. The most common ones are: penicillins, cephalosporins, fluoroquinolones, aminoglycosides, tetracyclines, macrolides, and polypeptides.
- Before the discovery of the antibiotic penicillin, infection was a leading cause of death.
- A broad-spectrum antibiotic kills many kinds of bacteria, while a narrow-spectrum antibiotic kills only a small variety of microbes.
- Broad-spectrum antibiotics used to treat bacterial infections can also kill beneficial bacteria found in the skin and in the digestive system. These "friendly" bacteria protect against yeast, fungal, and other kinds of infections.
- Antibiotics are usually taken by mouth, but can be given intravenously (through a vein), injected into a muscle, or applied on the skin.
- Green tea can increase the bacteria-killing properties of antibiotics, according to a study by researchers at Alexandria University in Egypt.
- The most frequent allergic reactions to antibiotics are skin rashes and digestive tract disorders.
- Penicillin is the leading cause of anaphylactic shock, a severe and life-threatening allergic reaction.

Antibiotic Use

The Centers for Disease Control and Prevention (CDC) has made the following statements:

- Two million pounds of antibiotics were produced in the United States in 1954. By 2000 production had increased to over 50 million pounds.

- Antibiotics can stop bacterial infections, not viral infections. Yet more than 50 percent of antibiotics are prescribed in doctors' offices for upper respiratory illnesses, which are most often caused by viruses.
- Fifty percent of patients who are given prescriptions for antibiotics do not need them.
- In the United States, three out of ten children who visit a health care provider for the common cold receive an antibiotic even though antibiotics are ineffective against the cold virus.
- Up to 70 percent of residents in nursing homes receive an antibiotic every year.
- Pigs and chickens are the primary receivers of antibiotics in the farming industry.

Most patients are prescribed antibiotics without the physician knowing the cause of the infection, according to Britain's National Health Service.

According to the World Health Organization (WHO):

- More than half of the world's antibiotics are used on farm animals.
- Over the past thirty years, the use of penicillin-type drugs in animals increased by 600 percent, and the use of tetracyclines increased by 1500 percent.

Antibiotic Resistance
- Bacterial drug resistance is a natural evolutionary phenomenon.
- According to the California Department of Health Services, penicillin-type antibiotics are not effective for one out of three patients.

According to WHO:
- Low-quality medicines, wrong prescriptions, and poor infection control contribute to the spread of bacterial drug resistance.
- Antibiotic-resistant strains of *Staphlycoccus aureus* (known as "MRSA") and various enterococci (intestinal bacteria) are common and pose a global health problem in hospitals.
- By 2011 over 60 percent of *Staphylococcus aureus* were resistant to several antibiotics.

- About 440,000 new cases of multidrug-resistant tuberculosis emerge each year, causing at least 150,000 deaths.

According to the CDC:
- The presence of antibiotic-resistant bacteria is greatest during the month following a patient's antibiotic use and may persist for up to one year.
- Antibiotics are a shared resource; the way they are used today in one patient directly impacts how effective they will be for other patients in the future.
- In the United States 250,000 nursing home residents have bacterial infections; 27,000 of them have antibiotic-resistant infections.
- The *New England Journal of Medicine* reports that 5 to 10 percent of patients admitted to hospitals acquire a bacterial infection during their stay.

Organizations to Contact

The editors have compiled the following list of organizations concerned with the issues debated in this book. The descriptions are derived from materials provided by the organizations. All have publications or information available for interested readers. The list was compiled on the date of publication of the present volume; the information provided here may change. Be aware that many organizations take several weeks or longer to respond to inquiries, so allow as much time as possible for the receipt of requested materials.

American Council on Science and Health (ACSH)
1995 Broadway, 2nd Fl., New York, NY 10023-5860
(212) 362-7704
fax: (212) 362-4919
e-mail: acsh@acsh.org
website: www.acsh.org

ACSH is a consumer education consortium concerned with, among other topics, issues related to health and disease. ACSH maintains the website HealthFactsandFears, which provides informational articles and health updates such as "FDA Antibiotic Regulations Under the Microscope," and "Incentives Mulled for Drugmakers to Target 'Superbugs.'" The ACSH homepage includes links to recent articles, editorials, and speeches on diseases, food safety, and pharmaceuticals.

Animal Health Institute (AHI)
(202) 637-2440
e-mail: rphillips@ahi.org
website: www.ahi.org

Founded in 1941, the AHI promotes research and development of needed veterinary innovations and advocates for medicines that boost health in food animals and ensure the safety of the food supply. The "Issues and Advocacy" tab at its website includes links to articles such as "Fact or Fiction: Common Antibiotic Myths" and the report "Animal Antibiotics: Keeping Animals Healthy and Our Food Safe."

Center for a Livable Future
Johns Hopkins University
Bloomberg School of Public Health
615 N. Wolfe St., W7010, Baltimore, MD 21205-2179
(410) 502-7578
fax: (410) 502-7579
e-mail: clf@jhsph.edu
website: www.jhsph.edu/research/centers-and-institutes/johns-hop
kins-center-for-a-livable-future

The Center for a Livable Future aims to develop and communicate information about the complex relationships among diet, food production, the environment, and human health. It advocates for an ecological perspective in reducing threats to public health and to promote policies that protect the global environment and the ability to sustain life for future generations. One of the center's areas of focus is antibiotic resistance and food production. To this end, its website provides links to research articles, reports, and editorials, including "The Rise of Antibiotic Resistance: Consequences of FDA's Inaction" and "Antibiotic Resistance: A Mulit-Billion Dollar Health-Care Crisis."

Centers for Disease Control and Prevention (CDC)
1600 Clifton Rd., Atlanta, GA 30333
(800) 232-4636 or (888) 232-6348
e-mail: cdcinfo@cdc.gov
website: www.cdc.gov

A branch of the US Department of Health and Human Services, the CDC serves as the national focus for developing and applying disease prevention and control, environmental health, and health promotion and health education activities designed to improve the health of people in the United States. A comprehensive A–Z index with fact sheets on antibiotics and antimicrobial resistance are available through its website.

Food Safety Consortium (FSC)
110 Agriculture Bldg., University of Arkansas, Fayetteville, AR 72701
(479) 575-5647
fax: (479) 575-7531
e-mail: dedmark@uark.edu
website: www.uark.edu/depts/fsc

Congress established the FSC, consisting of researchers from the University of Arkansas, Iowa State University, and Kansas State University, in 1988 through a special Cooperative State Research Service Grant. It conducts extensive investigations into all areas of poultry, beef, and pork production. The consortium publishes *Meat and Poultry,* a journal for meat and poultry processors, with links to articles such as "No Evidence That Eating, Handling MRSA-Tainted Food Ups Human Risk."

Infectious Diseases Society of America (IDSA)
1300 Wilson Blvd., Ste. 300, Arlington, VA 22209
website: www.idsociety.org

The IDSA is a group representing physicians, scientists, and other health care professionals who specialize in infectious diseases. Its purpose is to improve the health of individuals, communities, and society by promoting excellence in patient care, education, research, public health, and prevention as it relates to infectious diseases. The society publishes two scholarly journals: the *Journal of Infectious Diseases* and *Clinical Infectious Diseases.* IDSA's online index includes links to guidelines and statements such as "Antibiotic Resistance: Promoting Critically Needed Antibiotic Research and Appropriate Use ('Stewardship') of These Precious Drugs."

MRSA Survivors Network (MSN)
PO Box 241, Hinsdale, IL 60522
(630) 325-4354
e-mail: info@mrsasurvivors.org
website: www.mrsasurvivors.org

Founded in 2003, MSN was the first nonprofit consumer organization in the United States to raise the alarm about the MRSA epidemic and other multidrug-resistant bacterial infections. MSN partners with health care professionals, health care companies, and consumer advocates in its mission to stop MRSA-related infections and deaths. Its website provides information about community-acquired MRSA, MRSA in pets, MRSA in athletes, and related topics, as well as a link to stories written by MRSA survivors.

National Foundation for Infectious Diseases (NFID)
4733 Bethesda Ave., Ste. 750, Bethesda, MD 20814
(301) 656-0003
fax: (301) 907-0878

e-mail: info@nfid.org
website: www.nfid.org

The foundation is a nonprofit philanthropic organization that supports disease research through grants and fellowships and educates the public about research, treatment, and prevention of infectious diseases. It publishes a newsletter, *Double Helix*, and its website offers a "Related Links" feature that connects to resources on antimicrobial resistance and food-borne illnesses.

National Institute of Allergy and Infectious Diseases (NIAID)
Office of Communications and Government Relations
6610 Rockledge Dr., MSC 6612, Bethesda, MD 20892-6612
(301) 402-1663
fax: (301) 402-0120
website: www.niaid.nih.gov

The NIAID conducts and supports research to better understand, treat, and ultimately prevent infectious, immunologic, and allergic diseases. Infections and antimicrobial resistance constitute two of the NIAID's areas of research, and many resources and articles are available from the NIAID on these topics, including "Combating Drug Resistance with Basic Research" and "New Approach to Fighting Staph Infections." The website includes a searchable database with links to fact sheets and updates on bacterial resistance.

US Food and Drug Administration (FDA)
10903 New Hampshire Ave., Silver Spring, MD 20993
(888) 463-6332
e-mail: druginfo@fda.hhs.gov
website: www.fda.gov

The FDA's mission is to promote and protect the public health by helping safe and effective foods, drugs, and medicines reach the marketplace in a timely manner and to monitor such products for continued safety after they are in distribution. The administration's work is a blending of law and science aimed at protecting consumers. The FDA publishes the magazine *FDA Consumer*, as well as various government documents, reports, fact sheets, and press announcements. The index available at its website provides links to brochures on the judicious use of antimicrobials in farm animals.

For Further Reading

Books

Buhner, Stephen Harrod. *Herbal Antibiotics: Natural Alternatives for Treating Drug-Resistant Bacteria.* 2nd ed. New York: Storey, 2012. The author is an herbal expert who examines the roots of antibiotic resistance and explores the value of natural remedies for infectious illnesses.

DiClaudio, Dennis. *The Hypochondriac's Pocket Guide to Horrible Diseases You Probably Already Have.* New York: Bloomsbury, 2005. The author is a medical editor and humorist who offers informative and entertaining descriptions of several ailments, including bacterial illnesses such as leprosy, plague, and flesh-eating disease.

Drlica, Karl S., and David S. Perlin. *Antibiotic Resistance: Understanding and Responding to an Emerging Crisis.* Upper Saddle River, NJ: FT, 2011. Two public health investigators discuss the emergence and spread of antibiotic resistance. They also suggest ways to minimize antibiotic resistance and extend the life spans of current antibiotics.

Hausler, Thomas. *Viruses vs. Superbugs: A Solution to the Antibiotics Crisis?* New York: Macmillan, 2007. This book presents a history of bacteriophages (phages)—viruses that kill bacteria but not humans. With the increase in drug-resistant bacterial infections, phage therapy could prove to be the best alternative to antibiotic treatment.

McKenna, Maryn. *Superbug: The Fatal Menace of MRSA.* New York: Free, 2010. Using real-life firsthand accounts, a public health journalist tells the story of the spread of the antibiotic-resistant staph bacterium commonly known as MRSA.

Sachs, Jessica Snyder. *Good Germs, Bad Germs: Health and Survival in a Bacterial World.* New York: Hill and Wang, 2008. A science writer explores the benefits of antibiotics as well as the reasons why they are losing their effectiveness. She contends that pharmaceutical researchers should find ways to disrupt microbial processes rather than creating drugs that simply kill germs.

Schmidt, Michael A. *Beyond Antibiotics: Strategies for Living in a World of Emerging Infections and Antibiotic-Resistant Bacteria.* 3rd ed. Berkeley, CA: North Atlantic, 2009. A physician offers guidelines for people who would like to build and strengthen their immunity without antibiotics.

Spellberg, Brad. *Rising Plague: The Global Threat from Deadly Bacteria and Our Dwindling Arsenal to Fight Them.* Amherst, NY: Prometheus, 2009. An infectious diseases specialist explores the potentially deadly public health crisis of antibiotic-resistant microbes. He recounts the frustration that he and his colleagues have faced while attempting to treat untreatable infections and argues that new and effective antibiotics must be produced.

Periodicals and Internet Sources

AllAfrica.com. "The Hunt for New Antibiotics," June 29, 2012. http://allafrica.com/stories/201206291023.html.

American Council on Science and Health. "Antibiotics for Most Sinus Infections Are Anti-Effective," February 17, 2012. www.acsh.org /antibiotics-for-most-sinus-infections-are-anti-effective.

Bakalar, Nicholas, "Vital Signs Hazards: Drug-Resistant Infections Fall Nationwide," *New York Times*, July 10, 2012.

Bloom, Josh, and Gilbert Ross. "New Antibiotics, Stat!," *National Review Online*, December 21, 2010. www.nationalreview.com /articles/255420/new-vaccines-stat-josh-bloom.

Bloomberg, Lindsey. "Livestock on Drugs," *E: The Environmental Magazine*, May/June 2012.

Boytchev, Hristio. "Research Links Childhood Antibiotics, Obesity," *Washington Post*, August 22, 2012.

Brody, Jane E. "Popular Antibiotics May Carry Serious Side Effects," *New York Times*, Septermber 10, 2012.

Castillo, Michelle. "Less than Half of Americans Recognize Antibiotic Overuse as a Problem," *CBS News*, November 13, 2012. www .cbsnews.com/8301-204_162-57549178/less-than-half-of-ameri cans-recognize-antibiotic-overuse-as-a-problem.

Economist. "The Path of Least Resistance: Drugmakers and Antibiotics," May 12, 2012.

Eisler, Peter. "Drugs Can't Stop This Killer," *USA Today*, November 29, 2012.

Fabregas, Luis. "A Pill for Every Ill Is Dangerous Prescription," *Pittsburgh Tribune-Review*, May 26, 2012.

Glynn, Sarah. "Childhood Obesity Linked with Antibiotic Use in Infants Under 6 Months Old," Medical News Today, August 22, 2012. www.medicalnewstoday.com/articles/249289.php.

Grayson, Lindsay. "Smarter, Cleaner Approach Needed to Fight Superbugs," *Age*, July 14, 2012.

Harris, Gardiner. "New Prescription Requirement Will Cut Use of Antibiotics in Livestock, FDA Says," *New York Times*, April 12, 2012.

Interlandi, Jeneen. "Are We Running Out of Antibiotics?," *Newsweek*, December 13, 2010.

Lunau, Kate. "Superbug Meet Your Maker: Frogs Evolved to Fight Off Microbes." *Maclean's*, September 27, 2010.

Marinos, Sarah. "The Future of Antibiotics: The World Health Organization Has Warned That the Overuse of Antibiotics Is Creating Hard-to-Kill Bugs and a Potential Health Crisis," *Good Health*, August 1, 2011.

McArdle, Megan. "Resistance Is Futile," *Atlantic*, September 7, 2011.

National Hog Farmer. "NPPC Stands Its Ground: Antibiotic Use Aids Health," July 16, 2010.

Owen, Jonathan. "Antibiotics Losing the Fight Against Deadly Bacteria," *Independent* (London), September 18, 2011. www.independent.co.uk/news/science/antibiotics-losing-the-fight-against-deadly-bacteria-2356583.html.

Philadelphia Inquirer. "Drug-Fed Chickens Need to Go Cold Turkey," November 19, 2011.

Philpott, Tom. "Fat Pharm: Factory Animals Are Pumped Full of Antibiotics to Make Them Gain Weight. What Does That Mean for Our Waistlines?," *Mother Jones*, November/December 2012.

Raymond, Richard. "Antibiotic Discussion Requires Facts, Opened Mind," *Feedstuffs*, November 5, 2012.

Raymond, Richard. "Antibiotics and Animals Raised for Food: Lies, Damn Lies, and Statistics," *Food Safety News*, January 7, 2013. http://www.foodsafetynews.com/2013/01/antibiotics-and-animals-raised-for-food-lies-damn-lies-and-statistics/#.UWX3GKL5CSp.

Science Illustrated. "Everlasting Antibiotics: Scientists Have Identified a Class of Compounds That Could Improve Antibiotic's Effectiveness and Thwart Drug-Resistant Bacteria. How Do They Defeat the Microbes? By Confusing Them," May/June 2010.

Speer, Nevil. "Concern Isn't Meat, It's Resistance," *Feedstuffs*, June 25, 2012.

St. Louis Post-Dispatch. "Save Antibiotics for People, Not Poultry," July 22, 2009.

Stoppler, Melissa Conrad. "Antibiotics 101," MedicineNet.com. March 7, 2012. www.medicinenet.com/script/main/art.asp?articlekey=53075.

Taylor, Michael R. "We're Striking the Right Balance," *USA Today*, April 17, 2012.

Ubelacker, Sheryl. "Superbug Secrets Unearthed," *Globe and Mail* (Toronto, ON), April 13, 2012.

Vastag, Brian. "NIH Bacterial Outbreak Highlights Antibiotic Deficiencies," *Washington Post*, August 24, 2012.

World Health Organization. "The Evolving Threat of Antimicrobial Resistance: Options for Action," 2012. www.who.int/patientsafety/implementation/amr/publication/en/.

Websites

Centers for Disease Control and Prevention Get Smart Campaign (www.cdc.gov/getsmart). This page on the Centers for Disease Control and Prevention (CDC) website offers educational materials on appropriate antibiotic use as well as information sheets, brochures, quizzes, articles, and links to other resources on antibiotics.

NARMS: National Antimicrobial Resistance Monitoring System (www.cdc.gov/narms). NARMS is a collaboration among the CDC, the US Food and Drug Administration, and the US Department of Agriculture. The website features recently updated information on the food-borne bacterial illnesses associated with antimicrobial resistance.

World Health Organization (www.who.int/en). WHO, an arm of the United Nations, assesses health trends and provides leadership on global health matters. The "Health Topics" section of its website includes a page on antimicrobial drug resistance, with links to articles, bulletins, and other documents on this topic.

Index

Picture Credits

© AP Images/Matt Rourke, 103

© AP Images/Orlin Wagner, 33

© BSIP SA/Alamy, 47

© Gale, Cengage, 16, 23, 34, 48, 56, 67, 80, 88, 95, 100, 107, 113

© Sanjeev Gupta/EPA/Landov, 93

© Tony Hertz/Alamy, 38

© Wayne Hutchinson/Alamy, 29

© Richard Levine/Alamy, 108

© David Mack/Science Source, 87

© Medical-on-Line/Alamy, 68

© MedicImage/Alamy, 24

© Photo Researchers/Alamy, 15

© Prisma Archive/Alamy, 42

© Realimage/Alamy, 11

© RGB Ventures LLC dba SuperStock/Alamy, 55

© Science Source, 72, 82

© Carol and Mark Warner/Science Source, 76

© whiteboxmedia Limited/Alamy, 111